Three Minutes a Day

VOLUME 38

Other Christopher Books in Print

Better to Light One Candle
and other volumes in the
Three Minutes a Day
series

God Delights in You

THREE MINUTES A DAY
VOLUME 38

Dennis Heaney
President, The Christophers

Stephanie Raha
Editor-in-Chief

Margaret O'Connell
Senior Research Editor

Staff Contributing Editors
Umberto Mignardi
Nicholas Monteleone
Regina Pappalardo
Anna Marie Tripodi

Contributors
Joan Bromfield
Monica Ann Yehle-Glick
Eileen Nagel
Jerry O'Neil
Karen Hazel Radenbaugh
Tanya Thurman
Anne Marie Welsh
Debra Yoo

The Christophers
12 East 48th Street
New York, NY 10017

Scriptural quotations in this publication are from the Revised Standard Version Bible, Catholic Edition, copyright 1965 and 1966 by the Division of Christian Education of the National Council of Churches of Christ in the U.S.A. and the New Revised Standard Version Bible, Catholic Edition, copyright 1989 by the Division of Christian Education of the National Council of Churches of Christ in the U.S.A. and used by permission.

Lead a life worthy of the calling

to which you have been called,

with all humility and gentleness, with patience,

bearing with one another in love,

making every effort to maintain

the unity of the Spirit in the bond of peace.

EPHESIANS 4:1 – 3

Introduction

Not long ago I was looking over the first edition of *Three Minutes a Day*. Published in 1950, it wasn't called Volume One or anything like that. No one–not even Father James Keller, the Maryknoll priest who founded The Christophers–had any idea at the time that this little book (subtitled "Christopher Thoughts for Daily Living") would be such a long-running best-seller.

Two passages from Father Keller's introduction to that original volume caught my eye. One of them explained that in offering an uplifting story and a brief prayer for each day of the year, the book reminded readers that they did not work alone, that "Christ works with and through each and every one who would be a Christopher."

Then, too, Father Keller's description of our organization was right to the point: "The Christopher movement has no chapters, no committees, no meetings. There are no memberships, no dues. Rather than having a large number of people 'paying dues and doing nothing', we have, from the beginning, set out to encourage tens of thousands to 'do something and pay nothing'."

Now we're up to Volume 38 of *Three Minutes a Day,* and after all these years both points still apply. Just as they did more than 50 years ago, our stories and our prayers remind us that we're all in this together. What's more, we still have no dues, no membership fees, no meetings. All that we ask is that Christophers everywhere "do something" to change the world. May the pages that follow encourage you to do just that!

Dennis Heaney
President, The Christophers

Many Ways to Make a Difference

"Each small step has a ripple effect," Betsy Taylor, executive director of the Center for a New American Dream, told *Woman's Day*. "In fact, if everyone picked just one thing to make this a better world, the impact would be staggering."

Here are some of their ideas to protect the environment:

- Ride your bike; skip just one car trip a week.
- Send fewer greeting cards but be creative, make your own cards, or use e-cards.
- Replace the four most-used 100-watt incandescent bulbs in your house with 23-watt compact fluorescent bulbs. The Alliance to Save Energy says the U.S. could save the energy produced by 30 power plants annually if each household did that.
- Reuse grocery bags, packaging materials.

Our world and our neighbors need our attention. Decide that this day—and this year—you will change things for the better.

(Jesus) said...It is written 'One does not live by bread alone, but by every word that comes from the mouth of the Lord'. (Matthew 4:4)

Creator, bless our stewardship of Earth's resources and creatures. Help us care for our neighbors.

Surprise!

Many people bring plants or flowers to create a cheery ambience when visiting relatives, friends and acquaintances who are hospitalized. But what about later on?

One day a few months after her discharge from the hospital, Elizabeth Cervone arrived home tired after a radiation treatment. She noticed a florist's van a few doors away and thought, "Some lucky person is receiving flowers, maybe for a birthday or anniversary."

Imagine Ms. Cervone's surprise two minutes later when she answered the ring at her door, and there stood the florist's delivery man. She said that the flowers really revived her spirits.

When at home recovering, people need to be reminded that they are in our thoughts and prayers. And, while we're on the subject, those providing care should be remembered, as well.

Do not hesitate to visit the sick, because for such deeds you will be loved. (Sirach 7:35)

Gracious Creator, remind me to share Your compassion with all—starting with those near and dear to me.

Finding Himself up a Creek

Nine years after John Beal returned to Seattle from Vietnam, he suffered three heart attacks in seven months. He was only 28. Doctors found that the decorated veteran had heart disease and post traumatic stress disorder and believed his next coronary would be fatal.

Leaving a hospital, Beal wandered to nearby Hamm Creek. The area had been made into a wasteland: a weedkiller, like the defoliant Agent Orange used in Vietnam, had destroyed everything green; garbage, not fish, filled the creek.

Beal had found his mission: restore the stream. He removed garbage from the creek; planted flowers, bushes and saplings; helped restock the waters with salmon. He also enlisted the aid of others.

Today, more than 20 years after he was told he would die, Beal lives—as do the great-great-great-grandchildren of the first two salmon he put in Hamm Creek.

What good work can add life to your life?

Prepare the way of the Lord. (Luke 3:4)

Show me Your face, Lord of Creation.

Signs of God on the Road

Mary Catherine and David Compton recall the first church sign that caught their attention. That message, in front of a North Carolina church, read: "Forbidden fruit creates many jams."

From that day on, the couple kept a notebook in their car to jot down these "sentence sermons" wherever they traveled, eventually publishing them in a book, *Roadside Church Signs Across America*. They write: "The signs make you think. They make you smile. They beg to be told and retold." Here are a few:

- "A sunrise is God's way of telling the world to lighten up."
- "God answers knee mail."
- "Don't give up—Moses was a basket case, too."
- "Lord, help me to be the person my dog thinks I am."
- "We aren't Dairy Queen but our Sundays are great!"
- "Life is fragile—handle with prayer."

The Lord is merciful and gracious. (Psalm 103:8)

I find signs of Your mercy and love all around me, Father, and I give You thanks.

Ethics in Business

For years, small-business owner Judy Wicks had admired the socially responsible business practices of ice cream maker Ben and Jerry's. When a large conglomerate took over the company, she was more determined than ever to preserve and promote the ethical management of small businesses.

The Philadelphia entrepreneur began organizing. She rallied small, progressive businesses like hers to build what she terms "a network of local, living economies" that serve the human and natural communities in their own backyard.

"Good business is not about money. It's about authentic relationships with your customers, employees and suppliers," she says. "Business is beautiful when it's a vehicle for the common good," she adds.

Can your work be more geared toward the common good?

Strive to make your efforts not just successful, but also ethical and beneficial to others.

Find enjoyment in all the toil with which one toils. (Ecclesiastes 5:18)

Holy Spirit, help guide me to find work that is meaningful and that edifies others.

Today's Teens, Tomorrow's Leaders

With all of the negative media stories about teens, it's easy to think that the young people of today won't amount to anything tomorrow. Think again.

The members of the St. Therese Youth Group in New Jersey are just one example of doing good. They use their musical talents to sing during Mass, meet to discuss current issues and volunteer for causes like cancer research fund-raisers and Habitat for Humanity projects. By helping those in need, these teens are becoming leaders.

More than anything, they have a place to go to find God, true friends and themselves. One member says, "I now know more about my religion and myself, and I'm a better person for it."

Take the time to see for yourself what young people are doing in your community. And encourage the teens you know to reach out to their neighbors in need.

May our sons in their youth be like plants full grown, our daughters like corner pillars, cut for the building of a palace. (Psalm 144:12)

Jesus, help keep today's youth true to Your ways.

The Price of Long Pants

Growing up in the Bronx during the 1930s, John Keith, like most boys his age, wore short pants or knickers. But when he was to graduate from elementary school, he learned that he was expected to wear long pants for the ceremony. He was even due to receive an academic award, adding to his desire to be well-dressed.

The problem was that Keith's family couldn't afford the new pants. Still, seeing how upset her son was by his predicament, Keith's mother promised to figure out a solution.

The next Saturday, Keith and his mother rode the trolley to the local shopping district, where they purchased a pair of tailored wool trousers for $3.50. On the trip home, however, Keith noticed that his mother's gold wedding band was missing. She had pawned it to buy the pants that meant so much to her son.

Love can lead to great sacrifice. What are you willing to give?

Better is a dinner of vegetables where love is than a fatted ox and hatred with it. (Proverbs 15:17)

Lord, please help us to recognize and respect the sacrifices of those who love us.

Alphabet Soup

Keri Linas, writing in *Family Circle* magazine, put together a page-long alphabetical list of words to describe herself. Here are some of them:

Adventurous. Blessed. Creative. Determined. Eloquent. Feisty. Genuine. Honest. Insightful. Joyful. Knowledgeable. Loving. Motivated. Natural. Original. Persistent. Quirky. Reliable. Spiritual. Trustworthy. Understanding. Versatile. Whimsical. FleXible. Youthful. Zany.

What might your personal alphabet look like? Find uplifting, positive words to describe the person you are and to celebrate all that is good about you. Or, select words that characterize the kind of person you would like to become. Put them on your mirror and tuck them into your wallet.

Consider why you admire these traits, and work to incorporate them into your daily life.

In the beginning was the Word, and the Word was with God, and the Word was God. (John 1:1)

Help me to be mindful, Holy God, of the power and responsibility I have for setting the tone of my life.

Challenges Welcome Here

Most of Terri Nalls' students couldn't read the billboard proclaiming Tifton, Georgia, "TURF GRASS CAPITAL OF THE WORLD," much less an entire book. So the teacher contacted Mike Brumby, head of Tift County's Foundation for Educational Excellence, and asked him to help her buy a software–based reading program. By year's end, the 400 Spencer Elementary School students had devoured 25,000 books.

This prompted Brumby to propose a billboard declaring, "WELCOME TO TIFTON, READING CAPITAL OF THE WORLD." With the county's literacy rate at only 40 percent, everyone thought he'd gone mad. But he believed if students could develop a passion for reading, so could the rest of the folks. A banner outside the library tracked progress toward their goal of 1,000,000 books.

Asked how they know they've read more books per capita than any other town, Brumby says, "We don't, but we welcome all challenges. The idea was to teach a love of books to children, and we've done that."

For God all things are possible. (Matthew 19:26)

Remind me, Lord, that through faith in You all things are possible.

Organic Urban Gardens

The financial crisis in Argentina caused the Buenos Aires Board of Education to sponsor a program teaching children about the benefits of gardening.

170 schools already have organic vegetable gardens. The federal government contributes gardening tools and instructors.

The program teaches the value of self-sufficiency to children and also to the parents who joined in to help. Community groups, senior citizens and some local hospital workers joined the original project. This made extra food available for a large number of soup kitchens.

Vegetable gardens in schools near slums became a source of food for the poor. In addition urban children are learning about the farming tools and techniques common in rural areas.

Originally initiated to help those in need, the program is a good reminder that creativity can help solve problems.

To each is given the manifestation of the spirit for the common good. (1 Corinthians 12:7)

Abba, help us remember to give thanks—and assistance.

Getting Through the Big Stuff

In his book *What About the Big Stuff?* Richard Carlson offers five principles to get through the tough times:

1. Skinned knees heal themselves. Just like the knee that makes its own scab, rely on your inner strength to see you through to a brighter tomorrow.

2. Measure twice, cut once. With a clearer, quieter mind, you'll be more effective in life and at making life's decisions.

3. Don't honk at the slow guy. Patience enables you to have the presence of mind to stay calm in a crisis.

4. Learn to love the rain. Our thinking, not our circumstances, creates much of our stress. So when the rain falls, take a deep breath and keep going.

5. Celebrate silence. Become a good listener. It lets you gather information, reflect on it and respond appropriately.

One more thought: PRAY.

God of my ancestors...who...have formed humankind to...rule the world in holiness and righteousness...give me the Wisdom that sits by Your throne.
(Wisdom of Solomon 9:1, 2, 3, 4)

Father, You are my hope.

When Worlds Connect

"Growing up in Memphis, I had a teacher in grade school who believed that every child could change the world," says Lisa Navarra. "I've carried her words with me all my life."

Navarra is today the associate director for Youth and Children's Ministries at St. John's Episcopal Church in McLean, Virginia. Each day she brings together low-income teens from Washington, D.C.'s Macfarland Middle School and teens from the affluent, largely white community of McLean for educational, social and cultural activities.

"When kids from D.C. come into the program, they think they're completely different from the kids who live in McLean, and vice versa," says Lisa. "But when the kids get on the basketball court or play volleyball together, they realize their similarities outweigh their difference and that their differences can help them broaden each other's worlds."

Young people can change the world—just look at Lisa and the teens in her care.

Train children in the right way. (Proverbs 22:6)

We are united in You, Lord. You are the source of all life and goodness.

Help and Hospitality

High in the Alps, Augustinian monks offer travelers welcome and, if necessary, rescue.

Founded in 1050, the Hospice du Grand-St.-Bernard is famous for its hospitality. The community first bred the noted Saint Bernard dogs in the 1600s to help in rescue work. Nowadays they only raise pups for sale.

But the monks, all trained mountaineers, continue to "welcome, succor, be attentive to every person, to anticipate their needs." That's true whether someone needs help traversing the perilous, often snow-bound pass between Switzerland and Italy or a person comes for a brief spiritual time out.

Each human life is full of perilous passes through rugged mountains of change, loss, loneliness, health problems, pain and ageing. Offering others comfort is a good way to make your own passage easier.

Comfort My people, says your God. Speak tenderly to Jerusalem...that she has served her term, that her penalty is paid. (Isaiah 40:1-2)

Merciful Savior, who needs a comforting word; a shoulder to lean on; a sheltering hug?

Through the Eyes of an Artist

In the 1940's, then 20-year-old Mary Keefe was asked to pose for a Norman Rockwell painting. The telephone operator who went on to become a dental hygienist agreed to the $5 per session fee and sat twice for the artist.

"Rosie the Riveter," became one of Rockwell's most famous *Saturday Evening Post* covers. Rockwell's masterpiece, created to salute women and their work supporting America during World War II, depicts a hefty woman in overalls, a rivet gun on her knees, as she eats a sandwich.

Rockwell called Keefe when he finished the picture and told her she was not going to like him when she saw the painting. Keefe's response? Although folks kidded her about being "Rosie" and she never saw a resemblance, she felt it had been a privilege to sit for Rockwell.

Every woman—and man—is blessed by God with abilities and the potential to contribute to society—and to fulfill her or him self.

A capable wife...works with willing hands... girds herself with strength, and makes her arms strong...strength and dignity are her clothing. (Proverbs 31:10, 13, 17,25)

Enable each of us, Holy God, to stay open to the possibilities You put before us.

The Link between Ignorance and Bigotry

It's no surprise that people targeted by negative stereotypes can be damaged by them. But researchers have determined that those who perpetuate these stereotypes can suffer intellectual and emotional impairment as well.

In a study whose results were published in the *Journal of Experimental and Social Psychology,* it was found that students who used stereotypes to describe a fictitious student they believed was African-American scored lower on a math test compared with students who did not use stereotypes. Further studies have indicated that when the stereotype of the elderly was involved, participants in that study walked more slowly.

It doesn't take more than common sense to realize that racism, or any "-ism," for that matter, breeds ignorance. Bigotry hurts the perpetrator as well as the victim.

Haven't we all learned that the best way to relate to one another is without preconceived notions and beliefs based on stereotypes? Let's rejoice in the differences among us.

Do not judge by appearances. (John 7:24)

Lord of all, guide me towards love and respect for all.

"All Are Significant"

While a student in nursing school, Joann Jones learned a lesson about the importance of every person.

In a letter to *Guideposts* magazine, Jones told about a professor who gave a surprise quiz one day. The student nurse did fine until the last question stumped her. It read: "What is the first name of the woman who cleans the school?" Like most of her classmates, she left it blank.

When asked about it, the professor admonished the students, "In your careers, you will meet many people. All are significant. They deserve your attention and care, even if all you do is smile and say 'hello.'"

Joann Jones never forgot that lesson–or that the woman's name was Dorothy.

Pay attention to all the people around you because they have a right to be recognized as unique individuals. Part of your own uniqueness is expressed in the way you treat others.

In everything do to others as you would have them do to you; for this is the Law and the Prophets. (Matthew 7:12)

Holy Spirit, I want other people to see my individuality. Please help me reciprocate with each man, woman or child I meet.

Creating a Vision

Bryan Bell is passionate about architecture done in a certain way. For some architects, Bell says, "design is about materials and space. For me, it's about the people who will inhabit the space."

Bell wants to create housing for America's migrant workers that is responsive to their real needs. For example, as the result of talking and listening to farm workers Bell designed a house with a sink on the porch. The workers wanted a place to wash off pesticides before entering their homes.

In another instance, Bell designed housing with bedrooms for husbands and wives, in addition to standard dormitories.

Passionate in his belief that architects need to value human beings as well as architectural form, he now teaches at North Carolina State University. He wants students to share his views on the importance of people and their needs.

Respect the needs of others–and your own.

I have set you an example. (John 13:15)

God, show professionals how to use their skills for the good of others and for Your glory.

You've Got to Have Friends

Study after study has shown that people with solid social networks–*people with friends*–have a better chance of surviving life-threatening illnesses; have stronger immune systems; improved mental health; longer lives.

But how can you stay connected when schedules make it tough to make time for pals? Sociologist Jan Yager, author of *Friendshift*, offers these tips:

- Use e-mail or instant messaging to stay in touch.
- Meet for coffee or a walk *before* work.
- Schedule a regular "Friends Time Out" to catch up with buddies.
- Invite a friend to share activities that you normally do alone, like exercising or doing errands.
- Try to be there for key events in your friend's life.

Your presence as a *friend*–and the presence of *friends*–will make a difference.

Happy is the one who finds a friend.
(Sirach 25:9)

I see You, Father, in my friends. Bless them.

Engineering Freedom

"The Underground Railroad seems to incite the imagination of people of all races," says Temple University history professor Charles Blockson. "It conjures up images of soft knocks on doors, whispers, trapdoors...intrigue, suspense and heroes of all races."

Many communities are working to preserve the last vestiges of this "railroad"–a network of safe houses and trails that formed an escape route for Black slaves from the South to the North. It's a difficult task. The secretive nature of the network that existed for years before the Civil War makes it hard to separate legend and fact. But historians and preservationists are beginning to match diaries, letters and newspaper accounts with oral histories.

What is it about the Underground Railroad that interests so many? Perhaps it is the brave selflessness of those who risked their lives for others' liberty.

How are you called to be brave in liberty's cause today?

(Jesus) found the place where it was written: "The Spirit of the Lord...has anointed me to... proclaim release to the captives." (Luke 4:18)

Jesus, remind me that either all are free or all are enslaved. Then strengthen me to stand up for my own freedoms and others'.

Double Dare

"Life is either a daring adventure or nothing," said Helen Keller. Growing up deaf and blind, Keller's own life demanded a spirit of courage.

Here are some suggestions for courageous living:

- Adopt a corner of your neighborhood to watch over.
- Stretch your mind–read a book you normally wouldn't.
- Say yes.
- Apologize.
- Do something that you fear.

Aviator Jacqueline Cochran says she has found adventure in flying, in world travel, in business and close at hand. "Adventure is a state of mind and spirit," she believes.

Adventure isn't where you find it. It's where you live it.

Render service with enthusiasm. (Ephesians 6:7)

Free my heart, God, to embrace the fullness of the adventure in my life.

Help on Wheels

You might call Thomas Weller an angel of the highway. His mission in life is to help motorists with flat tires, clogged fuel pumps or empty gas tanks.

Weller, a married father of two adult children, lives in El Cajon, California, and uses a 1955 Ford station wagon with 500,000 miles on it for his road rescues. The reason behind his Good Samaritan chores? When he was 16, his car slid off a highway. Hours later, a stranger towed him out and refused to accept any money. Instead, he told Weller that if he wanted to repay him, he could do so by passing the favor along to others.

That's just what Weller has done, some 3,000 times. He gives each motorist that he helps a card that reads, "I ask for no payment other than for you to pass on the favor."

Today, don't miss an opportunity to pass along a good word, a gesture or a favor to a stranger.

A man was going down from Jerusalem to Jericho, and fell into the hands of robbers...a Samaritan...when he saw him was moved with pity. (Luke 10:29, 33)

Spirit, instill in me the grace and goodness to serve others.

When the Wind's Knocked Out of You

The idea of sitting in a chair lift with her legs dangling free frightened nine-year-old Alice and kept her from the ski slopes.

But when she learned that the beginner hill offered a conveyor belt to tow her to the top, she agreed to try it.

Still, Alice was nervous and asked her instructor some questions before her trip uphill.

"What if I fall off?" she demanded of him.

"I've never fallen off," he answered matter-of-factly.

"But what would happen?"

"You'd have the wind knocked out of you."

Later, after an exhilarating day on the slopes, she told her family, "When I knew I wouldn't die if I fell off, then it was okay." Just having the wind knocked out of her was not enough to keep Alice from trying something new.

What mountain are you facing? Maybe you're worrying more than necessary. Maybe it really is a molehill after all.

Though I walk through the darkest valley, I fear no evil; for You are with me. (Psalm 23:4)

Don't let unfounded fears keep me from living life to the fullest, Loving Father.

Selling School

Donna Meade-McMillan loves her job and knows she makes a difference every day.

Executive director of the Paterson, New Jersey, Diocesan Scholarship Fund, Ms. Meade-McMillan raises money to help low-income parents pay their children's elementary and high school tuition.

Although fund raising is challenging work, she finds it exciting. She sees her job as giving "those less advantaged the same educational opportunities as those who can afford to pay private tuition costs." Donna Meade-McMillan added that parents become involved and "work together with us to give their kids a chance to move out of poverty."

It's wonderful when former students return to say how a good teacher made their lives better. Work that changes lives is ideal.

A disciple is not above the teacher, but everyone who is fully qualified will be like the teacher. (Luke 6:40)

Lord, help me to make a positive difference in someone's life today.

Saving the World over a Cup of Coffee

For drinkers of the Pura Vida brand of coffee, that first sip of java each morning is more than just a jump-start to the day. It's a way to send hope to poor children in Costa Rica.

John Sage and Chris Dearnley, company founders, first met at Harvard Business School. After graduation, the two went their separate ways. Dearnley eventually became an ordained minister, working in Costa Rica.

When the two got together, Dearnley would talk about his work with the poor. It was during one of those chats over fine Costa Rican coffee that they came up with the idea of a coffee business that would also support Dearnley's ministry.

"Not only are we seeking to reach into communities in need," Dearnley says, "but at the same time, coffee itself as a product is very communal. It's over a cup of coffee that hearts are opened and lives are shared."

Share your ideas and your heart with others.

Do not neglect to do good and to share what you have. (Hebrews 13:16)

Open our hearts, Father, so that we might share Your love this day.

Potluck Philanthropy

By adding a creative twist to their routine potluck suppers, a group of friends has been able to help others who are less financially fortunate.

Clinical psychologist Lisa Herrick hosted the dinners for her women friends. One, Dr. Amy Kossoff, spent her own money to help poor patients pay for a prescription or the rent.

So the potluck participants decided to donate $35 – "about what we would spend on a dinner out," said Dr. Kossoff – as well as a dish. After one potluck dinner Dr. Kossoff had $3,000 in donations.

Another diner, Anne Wallace, persuaded a bank to set up a free checking account for the group, now named Washington Womanade. Although disbursed in small amounts, the money makes a big difference for Dr. Kossoff's homeless, often mentally ill, marginally employed patients.

Generosity added to creativity can do wonders.

Those who are generous are blessed. (Proverbs 22:9)

Thank You, Lord, for generous, caring souls.

A True Hero

Paterson, New Jersey, fireman Anthony Camal was justifiably proud of winning a gold medal in judo in the World Police and Fire Games. After all, the 40-year-old had trained for that moment since he was six.

But a few weeks later, Camal faced a more important–and dangerous–challenge when he saved an 82-year-old man who was trapped in a fiery apartment building. To do so, he had to carry the man down three flights through smoke and intense heat, lugging 70 pounds of gear in the process.

"The judo competition was for me," Camal commented. "But in any one lifetime, how often are you going to be able to save someone's life?"

Perhaps we will not be pressed to save someone, but surely each of us can make a positive difference in another's life. Seek ways to do so each day.

Consider how to provoke one another to love and good deeds. (Hebrews 10:24)

Father, I will look to contribute to the greater good.

Freedom to Forgive

"Forgive and forget" may be a time-honored cliché, but the idea of truly forgiving and forgetting a hurt is largely unrealistic, says Sandra Lamb, in *Family Circle* magazine.

Experts she consulted said true forgiveness requires an enormous amount of patience as well as a commitment to resolve the conflict or issue. It does not require excusing or condoning offensive behavior, nor does it indicate weakness.

On the contrary. Dr. Robert Enright, an educational psychologist at the University of Wisconsin, calls forgiveness a great act of courage.

Interestingly, Lamb notes that it is possible to resolve grudges even if the offender does not acknowledge the offense. She points out that the act of forgiveness itself benefits both the person who is forgiven and the person who forgives.

Choose to forgive. And ask to be forgiven.

One who forgives an afront fosters friendship, but one who dwells on disputes will alienate a friend. (Proverbs 17:9)

Holy Spirit, help me not to waste time and energy brooding over offenses.

Stars in the Night Shift

John Granucci was just starting his career as a nurse when a spot opened up in orthopedic surgery. It would take him from part-time to full-time status and offer managerial experience, but it meant working the graveyard shift.

He took the chance and became the nurse in charge from 11 p.m. to 7 a.m. Back to working days, he is now the nurse in charge of the critical-care unit, a position that would not have been possible without his experience working nights.

A recent survey indicated that more people than ever go to work after dark. The U.S. Department of Labor's 2001 statistics show 9.7 million Americans work full-time evening or night shifts, up from 8.9 million in 1997. Nighttime posts often pay a bit more and offer career boosts often not found during daylight.

Some opportunities come to light in the dark. Wherever you find them, use them well.

Nothing is hidden that will not be disclosed. (Luke 8:17)

In times of distress, I call to You, Father. Light my path that I may find my way to You.

Golden Flowers

Vonetta Flowers always wanted to be an Olympian. Unfortunately, she was still recuperating from ankle surgery during track and field qualifying rounds for the 2000 Summer Olympic games. She did not make the team.

Flowers' husband then saw a flier advertising for athletes interested in becoming bobsledders. Flowers auditioned and was invited to Germany where she would see her first bobsled.

After navigating the sticky politics of a sport in which pilots frequently fire brakemen, Flowers and the pilot, Jill Bakken, headed for the Salt Lake City Olympics as the underdogs. But the two of them brought home the gold.

Flowers not only realized her Olympic dream, she became the first African-American to win a Winter Olympics medal. Her path to victory was simply a little different from the one she had envisioned.

Two are better than one, because they have a good reward for their toil. For if they fall, one will lift up the other. (Ecclesiastes 4:9-10)

Remind me, God, that Your hand is guiding me, even when I feel lost.

Will Power

Will Power to Youth is an organization that helps teach teenagers job skills and life values using the plays of William Shakespeare.

Two California performing artists, Dani Bedau and Ben Donnenberg, founded the group in the wake of racial unrest after the 1992 Rodney King beating. The program helps broaden horizons for low-income youths. Many teens find it boosts their self-confidence and encourages them to respect others and to value differences. In addition they learn important job skills.

The group studies a Shakespearean play, then writes and performs a fully staged adaptation. Youngsters earn wages and receive school credit.

Working in the group was a positive experience for Rudy Lopez, 17, who discovered that he had acting ability. And he learned to take time to understand another person's point of view.

"Will Power opens your eyes," said Lopez. "It helps you understand the world around you."

Understanding is effective.
(Wisdom of Solomon 8:6)

Holy Spirit, inspire us to guide our young people.

Celebrating Ourselves and Others

Tolerance, acceptance of differences, rejoicing in our Creator's obvious delight in diversity, is the foundation of peace–personal, familial, communal, national, international.

All U. S. citizens, except Native Americans, are immigrants or are descended from them. As a family project, research your own country or countries of origin. Read travel books or other literature, see a play or listen to music from or about the area.

Then learn about others. Once a month, visit an ethnic restaurant. Afterwards help the children find that nation on a globe or map. As a family, read about its history, peoples and culture and listen to music from that country, too. Visit exhibits of ethnic art and culture at museums.

Find out about national or ethnic holidays such as Chinese New Year, Bastille Day, Cinco de Mayo, Epiphany or Los Tres Reyes, Kwanza. If there is a public celebration, go to it.

Celebrate diversity. Teach tolerance. Make peace.

Have we not all one father? Has not one God created us? (Malachi 2:10)

Creator, forgive us our prejudices. Teach us respect.

Secret Code to Freedom

Graduating with a "D" in history from New Orleans' St. Augustine High School, Raymond Dobard certainly didn't appear to have a gift for the subject. But that was before he became excited by art and textiles–and how they were involved with the history of African-Americans.

He went on to earn advanced degrees before becoming an art history professor at Howard University. Dobard also co-authored a book titled, *Hidden in Plain View: A Secret Story of Quilts and the Underground Railroad*. It details how Africans enslaved in the United States often included secret codes within the design of quilts to guide others along the Underground Railroad.

Refuting the notion that slaves were a passive people who had to rely on whites to free them, Dobard's book suggests that slaves adapted to their situation, but communicated with each other using their own traditions. Quilts, for example, reflected African textile styles and customs.

Rather than judging too fast, search for others' potential.

Do not judge, so that you may not be judged. (Matthew 7:1)

Help me avoid judging others, Holy Spirit.

Springing Ahead

For Laura Ishler, spring comes in February. Moving spring back dates back to childhood days when she would help her grandfather order from the seed catalog. "He'd open the catalog and out would stream a rainbow of colors–bright orange pumpkins, fire red bushes, purple turnips and yellow string beans," Ishler remembers.

Ishler would carefully fill out the order form and then, "I'd tear down to his mailbox and brush the snow off...loosen the ice and pull up the red flag to signal the mailman to...take our envelope. That red flag...stopped winter."

Now, "every February, when I've had enough of the bone-chilling winter in...Pennsylvania, I sit down with the seed catalog. As I turn the pages, I can almost hear the snow melt and feel Grandpa smiling down from Heaven."

Who or what melts icy weather or icy situations for you?

Take My yoke upon you, and learn from Me...and you will find rest for your souls. (Matthew 11:29)

Season after season tells of Your marvelous works, Lord. May we come to know and appreciate these changes.

Coffee Finds Faith

On February 3, 1966, U.S. Navy Captain Gerald L. Coffee, flying a reconnaissance mission from the decks of the aircraft carrier *U.S.S. Kitty Hawk* off the coast of North Vietnam, lost control of the aircraft. Captured on the ground by North Vietnamese forces, he would spend the next seven-plus years in prison.

"The key to my survival, I realized, was faith," Coffee observes, "faith in God above all, but also faith in others and in myself.

"I learned to appreciate myself and my own humanness and learned to forgive myself for the first time," he adds.

Above all, Coffee's faith in God got him through those prison years. "The first two English words I scratched on my cell wall made all the difference," Coffee recalls. "Two words with an equal sign between them: *God = Strength.*"

Each of us, no matter what our circumstance, can find strength in God as we find Him in ourselves and in others.

Blessed be the Lord, my rock. (Psalm 144:1)

Increase my faith, Lord, so that I may not be anxious and fearful.

High-tech Debacles Teach about Life

Technological innovation isn't always a success. The more we innovate, the more ways there are to fail.

In London, the Millennium Bridge, the first footbridge ever built across the Thames, was closed within 72 hours of opening because it vibrated and bounced as people walked on it. Cause: "unintentional synchronization" when folks walked in step with the slight, expected sway of the bridge.

By its nature, innovation leads into uncharted territory where danger cannot be predicted. The good news is that as technologies have grown, so have expectations for safety. A crisis usually means that an appropriate response, including reform and regulation, will be developed.

Do you wait for a disaster to call on God? While problems are a natural part of life, if we trust God and turn to Him, we will be better able to deal with life's crises.

Ask, and it will be given you; search, and you will find; knock, and the door will be opened for you. (Luke 11:9)

Heavenly Father, may my faith in You mature as I remember to talk with You daily.

Mapping Your Way to Compassion

David Smith is a geography teacher who travels the world as a consultant, showing other educators how to encourage interest in physical geography, as well as an abiding respect for our fellow inhabitants of planet Earth.

In his book, *If the World Were a Village,* Smith puts global demographics on a scale that's easy to grasp by expressing it in terms of just 100 people. For example, 17 of those people can't read or write. 20 earn less than a dollar a day. 22 speak Chinese. 32 are Christians. 39 are 18 years old or younger. 50 are hungry some or all of the time and another 20 are severely undernourished.

Yet, David Smith believes that the most important lessons "are kindness, service, and radical thoughts like 'Look out for your neighbor'." Love of neighbor has always been radical enough to change the world.

The first (commandment) is...'love the Lord... with all your heart...soul...mind, and... strength'. The second...'love your neighbor as yourself'. (Mark 12:29, 30-31)

Spirit of Love, live in us Your people and help us see You in one another.

Community Building

Oxford, Mississippi, has progressed from the days when riots broke out because a black student wanted to register at the University of Mississippi.

Nowadays, Oxford is a popular place to visit due in no small measure to Richard Howorth, owner of Square Books, town mayor and former president of the American Booksellers Association.

Members of the association are generally independent bookstore owners who are part of their neighborhoods. In Oxford and elsewhere, before the domination of malls, people would go to the town square on Saturdays to get a haircut, buy local produce and listen to street-corner preachers. More than a marketplace, the town square was the center of community life.

Through readings, signings and its café, Square Books has helped breathe life back into its town square.

All of us experience the give-and-take of our neighborhood. But how much giving are we doing?

Old men and women shall again sit in the streets...and the city shall be full of boys and girls playing in its streets. (Zechariah 8:45)

Bless us, Lord, with the love and support of family, friends and a caring community.

Handling an Excuse-Maker

No matter how much you love someone close to you, if he or she is an excuse-maker it could easily drive you crazy. So, here are a few tips on maintaining your sanity:

- Don't pretend to believe silly excuses. There's no reason to be party to a lie.
- Don't put yourself in a position in which the person is likely to disappoint you. For example, if he or she is always late, go to the movies or theater with someone else.
- Losing your temper won't help because excuse-makers are used to people being angry at them. Let actions speak louder than words.

Life is short. Don't allow the chronic problems of others to ensnare you in negativity. And if you're the one always making excuses, it's not too late to change. Just don't let past mistakes be your rationale for future ones.

The righteous live by their faith. (Habakkuk 2:4)

Help me to forgive, Jesus, but to be no one's doormat.

Changing History on the Job

Major Charity Adams Earley commanded the only all-black Women's Army Corps unit, the 6888th Central Postal Directory Battalion, to serve overseas in World War II.

In 1996, she was finally honored for her wartime service. She said: "Students ask me, 'How did it feel to know you were making history?' But you don't know you're making history when it's happening. I just wanted to do my job."

"Doing her job" meant opposing segregation in the armed forces. In England, Major Adams refused Red Cross equipment for a segregated recreational center–her battalion was eventually allowed to use the same recreational center as whites–and she persuaded unit members not to stay at a segregated Red Cross hotel in London while on leave.

In life, each person can and should strive to overcome prejudice. We need to speak up not only on our own behalf, but also for others–that's "doing your job" as a human being.

Whose offspring are worthy of honor? Human offspring. (Sirach 10:19)

May my actions today reveal Your love, to all whom I meet, Father Creator.

Making It Through the Night

In the months after his mother's death, Jerry found himself awake, alone, in the early morning hours in the house they had shared. Not wanting to disturb his sister, Jerry found comfort in calling her office voicemail because her voice was so much like their mother's.

Loneliness, that empty feeling, especially after significant loss, can be devastating. There are ways to cope.

- Adopt a pet.
- Join a club.
- Smile! It puts others at ease, and makes you more approachable.
- Seek new friends.
- Care for yourself physically and spiritually.

When Jerry's sister discovered his early morning calls, she and her daughter began visiting him every Saturday. Jerry started eating with coworkers weekly. Though still alone in the early morning, Jerry had good times and people to help him through.

When the Lord saw her, He had compassion for her and said to her, "Do not weep." (Luke 7:13)

Lord, may I feel Your love and find my strength in You.

Cyberspace Sympathy

Today you can send an e-greeting card for every occasion from birthdays to bon voyage. But do some occasions like a death of a loved one make sending an e-card a social blunder?

Annie Scully had mixed emotions about receiving sympathy e-cards after her husband died of a heart attack. While she was "touched that people acknowledged my grief and loss" and felt "it was better to get some kind of communication than nothing at all," she admits that the cyber cards did give her pause.

Supporters of web cards say they are an easy, fun and efficient way to express feelings. Others say the relationship between the sender and the receiver determines the appropriateness of an electronic sentiment. As our world evolves, so does our etiquette, but sometimes the very effort behind a handwritten note makes a difference.

However you say it, let others know you're thinking of them–whatever the occasion.

**Greet one another with a holy kiss.
(2 Corinthians 13:12)**

May I find helpful words when my loved ones are in need, God.

The Silk Road Project

Internationally renowned cellist Yo-Yo Ma was born in Paris to parents who had emigrated from China. When he was seven, they moved to the United States. These days Ma has another passion besides music: the many cultures of The Silk Road Project.

Ma hopes to "study the flow of ideas… along the Silk Road," those caravan routes between the eastern Mediterranean and China from about 200 B.C. through the 1400s A.D. Music and musical instruments, foodstuffs, herbs, religions, gunpowder and printing presses, precious gems and fabrics moved over the road along with people and their cultures.

The Silk Road Project draws together musicians from the disparate cultures of the Silk Road countries to create a new global music using their native instruments. Films, storytelling, exhibitions, festivals and lectures also celebrate the peoples of yesterday and today.

Use your talents and passions to remind others of our common humanity.

The nations spread abroad on the earth after the flood. Now the whole earth had one language and the same words. (Genesis 10:32-11:1)

Creator, unite humankind in one search for lasting peace with justice.

How Will You Be Remembered?

Although Abraham Lincoln's inspiration will live for the ages, the last of his descendants actually died in 1985.

Only the President's oldest son, Robert Todd Lincoln, lived into adulthood. A Harvard graduate, he earned a fortune as a railroad tycoon and served his country as secretary of war in the 1880's and then as minister to England. He died in 1926.

It's possible to get a flavor of how the President's son and succeeding generations lived by visiting Hildene, Robert Lincoln's 24-room mansion on 412 acres in Manchester, Vermont. It's been restored and preserved for others to enjoy. The elegant house and its furnishings as well as the formal gardens are a far cry from the poverty of Abraham Lincoln's roots. Rather, the estate reflects Robert Lincoln's own history and fortunes.

What will you be remembered for? A question worth giving some thought to today.

In the memory of virtue is immortality. (Wisdom 4:1)

Inspire us, Holy Spirit, to leave a legacy of goodness.

Doctor on Call

Since 1990, Dr. Regina Benjamin has been the sole physician in the tiny, impoverished Gulf Coast town of Bayou La Batre, Alabama. She kept her first clinic going by working in emergency rooms and nursing homes. Then, while raising money for a new clinic after a hurricane, she treated her patients out of her 1988 Ford pickup truck.

The first African-American president of the Medical Association of the State of Alabama, Dr. Benjamin has won national recognition for her work on behalf of the rural poor. She is also held in high regard by her neighbors. Says one patient, she "is as good a person as she is a doctor."

She hopes to hire another doctor and already has the want ad: "Long hours, low pay, great job satisfaction and all the shrimp and oysters you can eat."

Money is certainly necessary, but there are greater rewards for making a difference, for doing good.

Help the poor for the Commandment's sake. (Sirach 29:9)

Let me not forget that money is far from everything, Father.

Second Chance for Romance

Sometimes a high school romance does work out—even if it takes a while.

Michael Applebaum and Carine Raimbaud fell in love as seniors at Lexington (Massachusetts) High School. But, Raimbaud was a French exchange student and went home at year's end. Applebaum pursued a career as a concert violinist; she as an attorney.

When Carine Raimbaud returned for a visit to the United States almost a decade later, she called her old friend. A year later, Michael Applebaum moved to Paris. They are now married and the parents of two sons.

"It had to happen this way," says Carine Raimbaud Applebaum. She believes their time apart gave them the necessary maturity to make their marriage work.

Not all good-byes are forever. Once in a while, life gives us a second chance that may be even better than the first.

The fruit of the Spirit is love, joy, peace, patience. (Galatians 5:22)

Holy Spirit, keep us from dwelling on disappointments. Help us realize that You give us amazing daily opportunities for faith, hope and love.

Are You In or Out?

Think back—were you one of the popular kids in school, one of the "losers," or like most, somewhere in between? Cliques begin in elementary school. The desire to fit in can help define, in both good and bad ways, a child's sense of self. How can you help your child cope?

- Children's feelings are real. Allow them to express frustrations without your "fixing" things. Be a good listener.

- Avoid judgments. Today's enemy could be tomorrow's best friend.

- Remind children that God values them as individuals. Make sure they know that you love them.

- Explain that even popular kids have insecurities. Dissect the clique myth.

- Teach about being a friend by being a good friend yourself. Go easy on advice.

We all like to be accepted by "the group," but it is our behavior as the individuals whom God created which defines us.

God created humankind...in the likeness of God. Male and female He created them, and He...named them 'Humankind'. (Genesis 5:1-2)

Jesus, please assure children, especially the unpopular ones, of Your love for them.

Prescription for Life

Medical students already know the pressures of anatomy tests, laboratory work, and marathon hospital sessions. But many medical schools are now advocating the addition of a clinical skills assessment test to the national medical licensing exam.

This means that soon-to-be doctors would be tested on their bedside manners. Role players trained to describe symptoms of various diseases and to act out their effects would rate the medical students on behavior including eye contact, body language, and the ability to explain things clearly. Senior doctors would grade the students based on the appropriateness of their diagnoses and the patient-actors' ratings.

A pilot program is already in place and, if successful, would become the standard to ensure better doctor-patient relations within a few years.

You may have the necessary skills to be successful. But how would you rate your communication skills with your colleagues and loved ones?

Speak out. (Proverbs 31:9)

Treat me mercifully, God, as I try to be merciful with others.

A Trophy Shared

Ray Bourque played a key role in capturing one of the most coveted awards in sports, the Stanley Cup, in June 2001. A well-liked and respected professional hockey player for 22 years, his yearning for the sport's top prize was shared by his many fans.

Everyone understood when Colorado Avalanche team captain Joe Sakic decided to forgo the traditional captain's spin around the rink in order to get the 34½-pound sterling silver cup into Bourque's hands as quickly as possible.

The following Monday morning, thousands showed up at Denver's Civic Center Park for a rally to celebrate the victory that was so long in coming.

No one is guaranteed success in anything, but each of us can know that when we've done our best, we've done all we can.

You are...members of the household of God, built upon the foundation of the apostles and prophets, with Christ Jesus himself as the cornerstone. (Ephesians 2:19-20)

Thank You, loving Father, for the joy we know in community—and in doing our best in all endeavors.

Waters of Hope in the Bronx

For more than 60 years, Our Lady of Lourdes Grotto in the Bronx, New York, has inspired hundreds of stories of blind people seeing, tumors shrinking and those in wheelchairs walking.

Every week hundreds line up to drink, to wash hands and faces and to fill containers with the water that flows from behind a statue of the Virgin Mary. It comes from the city water supply.

Most come to be cured. But after the terrorist attacks on the United States in September, 2001, "people were coming here for solace and consolation," says Michael Greco, a volunteer.

No one has investigated the cures credited to the grotto's waters; many people need no proof. "Some people will come and say this isn't real," offers Christina Mercora, 66, who has visited the grotto every week since she was a child. "But, for me, it is."

Faith and hope in God can be the heart of our comfort in hard times.

All those who had any who were sick..brought them to (Jesus); and He laid His hands on each of them and cured them. (Luke 4:40)

Heal me, Father, wash away my fears and doubts.

One Man's Key to Success

Guy Kawasaki, an Apple Corporation executive, offers these suggestions for business and for life:

- Ignore people's current status. It's narrow-minded, plus yesterday's subordinate may be tomorrow's peer.

- Help others. Don't do things for others to get something in return; offer to help because it's the right thing to do. The help you give today can come back to you in unexpected ways.

- Focus on little things: thank you notes, baby gifts, simple acts of kindness. You will be repaid countless times.

- There is enough good fortune to go around. Someone else's good luck doesn't take away from yours.

- Give back, whether through your church or through charitable organizations; to give is to receive.

Take your everyday chances to do good.

Bless your Maker who fills you with His good gifts. (Sirach 32:13)

Jesus, Your words serve as a guide to life. Thank You for Your precious teachings.

Hello? Can You Hear Me?

Remember when cellular phones were a rarity?

That's changed. Cellular phones are everywhere. In 2000, 36 percent of teens carried their own cell phone. Some estimate that by 2006, that percentage will jump to 75 percent. It seems the cell phone "customer" is getting younger still: it is not uncommon to see middle school students, cell phone in hand.

Some say cell phones are a boon to children and teens in the event of an emergency. Others see the rise in cell phone use as an alarming trend away from genuine one-on-one communication.

Funny how the very same item can serve to both connect and distance people. That's a reminder that life is full of paradoxes. There are usually at least two sides to every story.

Listen carefully. (Job 13:17)

Help me avoid rigidity in my thoughts and actions, Holy Spirit. Help me remain open to other people's views as well as their wants and needs.

Walking through Pain

A year after JoAnne Haverland took a job running the snack bar at a local private college, a secretarial position opened up in the admissions office. JoAnne applied and got the job.

Within a week, JoAnne's father was diagnosed with a brain tumor. "I was so emotionally distraught that I could not concentrate on what I needed to learn or do at my new job," JoAnne recalls. "It was all I could do to get through each day without making too many mistakes."

One day a co-worker, noticing JoAnne's anguish, invited her to go for a walk. "As I walked and sobbed, I choked out my feelings of inadequacy, frustration and pent-up pain," JoAnne recalls. "We walked for many blocks and, an hour later when we returned to the office, I was drained but renewed."

Sometimes when life gets tough, it's time to take a walk and have a talk with a friend.

Bear one another's burdens. (Galatians 6:2)

Wrap Your love around me in my pain, Father, so that I may bear that burden with renewed strength.

George Washington, Action Hero

When you think of George Washington do you envision a remote figure in a formal pose and powdered wig?

Organizers at Mount Vernon, Washington's home, are concerned with the diminishing role Washington is taking in the minds of many Americans. They're attempting to revive interest in the man who, almost through sheer force of will, helped form the United States of America.

As such, people who visit Mount Vernon now learn about the Washington who, as a frontier surveyor, was already famous by his mid-twenties. They learn about the general who shaped ragtag militias into an army that defeated the British war machine. And they learn about the warrior who, armed with only a sword, once rode at sixty Hessian mercenaries.

These stories are a far cry from the stuffy ideas many people have about America's Founding Fathers.

Try looking at something familiar from a different angle—you may be surprised by what you find.

Let us now sing the praises of...our ancestors... who...made a name for themselves by their valor. (Sirach 44:1,3)

Help us, Lord, to look beyond the obvious.

The National Story Project

When National Public Radio host Daniel Zwerdling asked novelist Paul Auster if he would become a regular storyteller for NPR's *Weekend All Things Considered,* the wordsmith was wary. Auster wasn't interested in producing fiction on demand, but to be polite, he agreed to consider Zwerdling's proposal.

It was Auster's wife who suggested soliciting stories from listeners. Intrigued, Auster agreed, and from that idea was born the National Story Project. After Auster asked listeners to send in their true stories, he was deluged with thousands, the best of which he read on *Weekend.*

Running the gamut from whimsical to tragic, the stories were so compelling that they led to a published anthology titled *I Thought My Father Was God.* The collection serves as "a museum of American reality," according to Auster.

We all have our stories to tell. Listen to others and share your own. It's all part of the human experience.

**Look closely and listen attentively.
(Ezekiel 40:4)**

Help us, Lord, to recognize the worth of our experience.

Patti's Pearls

"Don't try to change the wind, change the sails" and "Look at life through the windshield, not the rearview mirror" are among Patti's Pearls of Wisdom. Singer Patti LaBelle is surrounded by relatives who share nuggets of knowledge, which she has collected since childhood. Recently, the sayings began to take on more meaning than ever.

"Why have these pearls of wisdom suddenly become the blueprint for living my life?" she asks. Now in her mid-fifties, LaBelle says that the school of life has taught her a thing or two. "These timeless truths have made the greatest difference in my life," she explains. "They have either spared me a whole lot of pain and heartache, or could have, had I had the good sense to listen to them when they were first told to me."

Here's one more pearl: "The only time you run out of chances is when you stop taking them."

What have you learned from friends and relatives?

How attractive is sound judgment in the gray-haired, and for the aged to possess good counsel! (Sirach 25:4)

God above, open our hearts to wisdom, offered to us in so many surprising ways.

One Step at a Time

If you've felt overwhelmed lately, perhaps you need a new strategy. Consider these suggestions from Stephanie Denton:

- establish measurable goals
- make your goals challenging but not discouraging
- be sure your goals are yours, not someone else's

This method could be applied to many areas of your life. Perhaps, for example, your prayer life is not as rich as you'd like. Add a few minutes of quiet time each day, or take ten minutes of your lunch time to read inspirational materials.

Gradually you will notice that you are calmer and more focused. Even more significantly though, you will be increasingly aware of living in the presence of God.

The word about Jesus spread...crowds would gather to hear Him and to be cured...But He would withdraw to deserted places and pray. (Luke 5:15,16)

Merciful God, help me rest in the knowledge that I'm doing my best, if I am relying on You, helping my neighbors and fulfilling myself in Your service.

A Church Renewed

Beginning in May, 1945, at a prisoner of war camp in Umbarger, Texas, rations were drastically cut, as later documented by the International Red Cross. To keep their minds off food, the Italian POWs created paintings, sculptures and carvings.

Rev. John Krukkert of nearby St. Mary's Catholic Church was amazed by the beauty of the art. So he made a proposal: would the men decorate his all-white church in return for food? "In the bonds of Christian brotherhood and to the glory of God," they agreed. A portraitist, an interior decorator, a fresco artist, wood-carvers and stained glass makers set to work.

The women of St. Mary's Altar Society kept quantities of food coming while, six days a week, the Italian POWs painted and carved and installed magnificent stained-glass windows. They finished in 41 days.

This project did more than beautify a church and feed hungry men. It created a bridge of friendship.

What can you do to foster friendship?

Blessed are the peacemakers, for they will be called children of God. (Matthew 5:9)

Creator God, help me unearth my friends' hidden talents.

Justice in the Neighborhood

When the late Fred Rogers, longtime host of the children's TV series "Mister Rogers' Neighborhood," was invited to give the 2002 commencement address at Dartmouth College, a small but vocal number of students expressed disappointment. "I had hoped for someone more awe-evoking," said one.

Rogers, a Presbyterian minister, ignored the criticism and gave a thoughtful talk, even quoting one of the "neighborhood" songs, *It's You I Like,* adding, "I'm talking about that part of you that knows that life is far more than anything you can ever see or hear or touch.

"That deep part of you that allows you to stand for those things without which humankind cannot survive. Love that conquers hate, peace that rises triumphant over war, and justice that proves more powerful than greed."

That's a good reminder for young people starting out, as well as for those who have already traveled a long distance on life's road that passes through so many neighborhoods.

Love your neighbor as yourself. (Mark 12:31)

Loving Lord, show me how to be a good neighbor to all.

Children and Prayer

According to Annemarie Scobey-Polacheck writing in *St. Anthony Messenger,* "we often expect children to pray the same way adults do" instead of respecting their "stage of development ...(and) look(ing) for prayer experiences that fit the child."

Scobey-Polacheck makes these suggestions:

- pray often and spontaneously
- use concrete examples and images
- have a routine – say, prayer before and after meals; before bed time
- respect children's high energy levels
- attend weekly corporate worship
- give teens choices – how the family will pray, which service they want to attend
- be flexible, learning as you go along

And remember, good example works wonders.

(Jesus) took them up in His arms, laid His hands on them, and blessed them. (Mark 10:16)

Bless the children, Lord, as they come to know Your loving kindness.

Reconnecting With Your Faith

If you're a fan of Garry Trudeau's "Doonesbury" cartoons, you might know that the character of the red-bearded, idealist minister, Rev. Scot Sloan, is based on real-life minister Rev. Scotty McLennan, chaplain at Tufts University in Massachusetts.

The author of *Finding Your Religion: When the Faith You Grew Up with Has Lost Its Meaning*, McLennan believes that more than ever, people are seeking spirituality and a sense of balance and wholeness.

"In the long run I don't think spiritual depth is possible by grafting together different traditions that are not fully experienced or understood," he explains. "But I don't want people to think religion is all dour and sour. Have fun along the way."

Worship should contain a sense and experience of rejoicing. From baptisms to bar mitzvahs to youth rallies, rituals provide us a sense of community. Reconnecting to that sense of faith and community can bring substantial rewards.

When you come together...let all things be done for building up. (1 Corinthians 14:26)

Lord God, may public worship inspire and fulfill me.

Passing the Pooch

Shortly after Micaela Ward was diagnosed with leukemia, her doctor arranged for her to receive Melanie, a three-year-old Great White Pyrenees therapy dog.

One minor problem–Melanie the dog had to get from her Farmington, Maine, breeder to Micaela in Chadbourn, North Carolina.

Enter "The Hole in the Wall Gang," a charity that helps kids with cancer. They got in touch with Phi Kappa Tau, and east coast members of that fraternity organized a relay. "She jumped right in the front seat," says the first driver, Josh Masse, a Virginia Wesleyan sophomore. Three days and four hand-offs later, Matt McCuen, a Franklin & Marshall senior, put Melanie into Micaela's arms. "I had the best...I got to see her smile," he says.

Sometimes the seemingly impossible just requires a little teamwork and a lot of the right connections.

**Agree with one another, live in peace.
(2 Corinthians 13:11)**

In today's challenges, help me find Your strength in those around me.

Ask the Right Question

How do you make decisions?

There's no doubt that you have to make your choices in an imperfect world where all-too-often time is treated as a commodity, truth as flexible and fads as facts.

Sometimes you may feel compelled to make decisions without all the information you really need. At other times, you agonize endlessly rather than make a mistake.

Particularly when it comes to choices that involve moral issues, large or small, it isn't always easy. Still, it's up to us to use the reason God gave us, to decide as well as we can.

Consider something Martin Luther King, Jr., once said: "Cowardice asks the question, 'Is it safe?'; expedience asks the question, 'Is it politic?'; vanity asks the question, 'Is it popular?'; but conscience asks the question, 'Is it right?'"

You can't predict how things will turn out, but you can know you started with the right question.

Decide with equity. (Isaiah 11:4)

Holy Spirit, guide my mind and my conscience in facing facts and, always, in seeking Your will.

Pen Pals Meet At Last

Although Caren Gottesman had never met Carol Clarke, she says, "I cannot ever remember her not being a part of my life." It started when Gottesman, a 47-year-old mother of two, was a 10-year-old girl scout in New York corresponding with an overseas pen pal named Carol, who lived in Essex, outside of London.

Over the years their twice-monthly correspondence deepened as they shared the joys and heartbreaks of life. They also exchanged photos and occasionally spoke by phone. Finally, on the occasion of Gottesman's 25th wedding anniversary, she decided to go to London to meet Clarke.

Seeing each other at last, the two friends embraced, cried, swapped stories and shared gifts. Says Clarke, "After all these years, we couldn't help but be close."

Friendships are invaluable. Call or write a friend today.

Faithful friends are a sturdy shelter...a treasure...beyond price...life-saving medicine. (Sirach 6:14, 15, 16)

May I never take a friend for granted, Holy One.

"Jumbo-sizing" Our Diets

Small wonder—no pun intended—that Americans, especially children, are getting larger. The portions of food and drink are getting bigger and bigger, especially at fast food restaurants.

An example: McDonald's French fry portions. In the 1950s and '60s, the one size, which was just over two ounces, had about 200 calories. A decade later or so, a 320-calorie large size was introduced; in the 1980s the new "large," at 400 calories.

By the mid-1990s, "large" was eclipsed by "super size," for a mere 540 calories. By 2000, "large" had become "medium," and the new "super size" was seven ounces and contained 610 calories.

There's nothing wrong with enjoying French fries now and then. The key is moderation. Your heart and stomach will thank you for it.

And remember that moderation is generally good advice in most things. Give it a try.

Is not life more than food, and the body more than clothing? (Matthew 6:25)

Remind me to value quality over quantity, Divine Provider.

Leaving Your Mark

For someone who created grand entrances, he didn't have a grand exit. When Hector Guimard died in 1942 at age 75, much of his life's work went unacknowledged in his obituary. On the other hand, much of his work still exists and continues to delight.

In the early days of the 20th century, Guimard, who died in New York in 1942, designed and then constructed unique entrances to the Parisian subway system better known as Le Metro.

Clearly charmed by his creations, writer Edith Pearlman equates Guimard with Gustave Eiffel in that both "left the city of Paris permanently adorned." She says that the eighty-six entrances still in use can be seen as works of art with flowing ironwork. "Art nouveau architecture: romantic, abandoned, sensuous."

What evidence of your life's work will remain? How will you be remembered?

In the memory of virtue is immortality.
(Wisdom of Solomon 4:1)

May I do good work that benefits others, Father.

Friends: A Cause for Celebration

Find ways to celebrate the joys of friendship despite the demands of family and work. Here are some ways to see others:

- Dump the guilt. Since friends may help you be a better spouse, parent and person, they should occasionally take priority.
- Plan brief visits. Setting time limits encourages get-togethers. Ask friends, "Can we meet somewhere convenient for an hour?"
- Buy season tickets to an event or take a class or join a bowling league with a friend. You'll stay in touch and have fun.
- Go online. Sending e-mail is an easy way to stay connected.
- Volunteer at your church or local charity for work you can do together. This can add to your bonds of friendship.

Make friends. Then make time for them. Enrich your life.

Pleasant speech multiplies friends. (Sirach 6:5)

Teach us to nurture our friendships, Savior.

What Forgiveness Isn't and Is

Frederic Luskin asked, "Why do we allow someone who's nasty to us to rent so much space in our minds?" Why do we?

When you dwell on how someone has hurt you, you can forget what forgiveness is *not*. Forgiveness is not condoning, excusing, forgetting or denying a wrong. Nor does forgiveness mean continuing a relationship–marriage, friendship, work–that is abusive.

Forgiveness is acknowledging that you've been hurt. After that forgiveness means giving up resentment. The final step, being compassionate with the person who has hurt you, is the result of much patience toward self and much prayer for the offending party. So that's what forgiveness isn't and is.

Practice forgiveness now. Your blood pressure will be lower; your mood happier. Oh, and you will be making your world a bit brighter with forgiveness and mutual respect.

Do not judge, and you will not be judged; do not condemn, and you will not be condemned. Forgive, and you will be forgiven. (Luke 6:37)

Remind me, Jesus, that most people really are trying to do their best in every situation.

Heading Off Headaches on the Job

Between $5.6 and $17.2 billion. That's the estimated cost in lost productivity of migraine headaches to American businesses each year.

In a National Headache Foundation survey of working women migraine-sufferers, 89 percent have attacks at work. Some 55 percent report that migraines affect their ability to function at work, with 61 percent saying the pain forces them to take time off.

Employers are trying to cut their losses by introducing "Migraine Mentors at Work." Designed to educate people about migraine triggers and treatments, it includes workplace sessions with a physician which cover types of headaches, treatment options, preventive measures such as lifestyle modifications and where to turn for help and relief.

Education can make a huge difference in so many ways. Learn and teach, for your own sake and that of others.

Come, you that are blessed by my Father, inherit the kingdom...for...I was sick and you took care of me. (Matthew 25:34,35,36)

I sing of Your goodness, Creator, and praise You for all Your gifts.

Dispensing Solid Advice

"I think people who aren't positive don't succeed," Eppie Lederer once said. Of course, Lederer was better-known by her pen name, Ann Landers, and under that byline she spent nearly half a century guiding, advising and helping millions of readers.

Lederer counseled people in her column on just about every aspect of life and human relations. Said a fan, "If you had spent your life following her advice, you'd have worked out pretty well."

Not that she was immune to life's heartaches. She and her husband of 36 years split-up. When she told readers, "The lady with all the answers doesn't know the answer to this one," more than 35,000 letters of support arrived in her mail.

Yet for all the advice she dispensed, this lady who helped so many once declared, "I have received much more than I have given." Give and you too will receive.

Be rich in good works, generous.
(1 Timothy 6:18)

Father, may I be more a giver than a taker.

What To Do About Evil

"I view it as my job to tell people what can go wrong. If…I can't make a difference, I might as well go to the Cayman Islands and stick my head in the sand." Dr. Harvey Kushner, a Long Island University professor, is a terrorism expert who foresaw the day when America would be a victim of terrorism.

He is concerned about germ warfare. And he routinely notes unfamiliar cars loitering in his neighborhood. While some consider Kushner's interest in potential horrors "ghoulish" and "paranoid," he believes he is merely prudent. Especially since in referring to the world as his backyard, he says, "We live in a bad neighborhood."

But he also loves opera, art and chocolate, saying, "It's a way to balance the ugliness of what I have to think about in my job."

Since bad things do happen, we also must find a balance between useless worry and prudence; between acknowledgement of evil and appreciation of beauty.

Be courageous. (1 Corinthians 16:13)

Creator, give us the courage to face evil without giving up hope and a sense of wonder.

Nature is Wherever You Are

Diane Ackerman has traveled to the world's most exotic places. The author and naturalist has swum with whales off Patagonia and explored the coastal waters of the Antarctic.

However, equally as thrilling, she says, is the stroll through her own upstate New York garden.

"People think of nature as something we visit, when we are nature," she says. Ackerman says the loneliness felt in today's society comes from separation from nature, flowers, insects, which in essence separates us from ourselves. She believes that connecting with nature fosters intimacy among all living creatures, but unfortunately many people fear that connection.

Not ready to immerse yourself in wilderness? Ackerman recommends a daily walk, noticing the shape of clouds, the light gently resting on the trees, the earth's feel beneath your feet. It's a simple way to begin to restore your connection to nature, to yourself, to all creation and thereby to the Holy Spirit.

The earth is the Lord's and all...who live in it. (Psalm 24:1)

Lord of Lords, my thanks for our wondrous world!

The Family Way

My Big Fat Greek Wedding, a small budget movie that became one of the most profitable films of all time, obviously struck a chord with audiences. The story of Toula, a Greek-American, and her romance with a man who was not of Greek descent, touched themes that people of any heritage could understand.

It takes enormous strength for Toula to find her own way. At thirty, she still relies on her mother to talk her father into allowing her to take a few classes in computer technology.

Eventually, Toula's willingness to feed her soul in the way she knows is best for her opens the door to her life, preparing her heart to accept the possibilities of love.

"Don't let the past dictate who you are," a family member advises before the wedding. "But let it be part of who you become."

Do nothing without deliberation, but when you have acted, do not regret it. (Sirach 32:19)

Abba, help me preserve the best of my family's traditions while growing into the person You made me to be.

John Lewis: Man of Conscience

The civil rights struggles of the 1960s was violent but John Lewis wasn't. In 1961, Lewis was bloodied by a white mob for participating in the Freedom Rides, integrated bus rides through the South that tested a Supreme Court ruling on desegregating interstate transportation.

On March 22, 1965, Lewis led marchers across Selma's Edmund Pettus Bridge only to be "bludgeoned, gassed and charged" by mounted Alabama police. ABC television interrupted its Sunday night movie to air film of the violence.

Now a U.S. Congressman, Lewis continues to support causes from the environment to health care and campaign finance reform. His abiding philosophy is that life has a higher purpose. Men and women with "soul force" can and must do battle with oppressors, using nonviolent means.

Lewis says he is "not a hero." Let's just say he is a person who is guided by his conscience. Are you?

Cease to do evil, learn to do good; seek justice, rescue the oppressed, defend the orphan, plead for the widow. (Isaiah 1:17)

May we have the courage to lead a life of principle, Lord.

A Nurse with a Difference

As a parish nurse, Kathy Copak ministers to her patients' bodies and souls. Part of a small but growing group, she sees herself as a "pastoral partner" working with churches to provide holistic care to parishioners.

Copak assesses health status, takes blood pressures and consults other professionals. She also prays "with all the people I...see...that God will help us to get through in whatever way He wants."

One pastor believes Copak is in a unique position to develop trust with parishioners because she is a nurse. Another calls her a godsend.

For her part, Copak knows healing happens when she can "listen to what's going on in their hearts" physically and spiritually. She adds, "You are able to...touch people personally. ...That's what Christ did."

Who needs your caring, your concern, your prayers?

As you did it to one of the least...members of My family, you did it to Me. (Matthew 25:40)

Divine Healer, grant that others will find my presence healing.

A Case for Improvement

Charleston, South Carolina, is home to a booming tourist industry. However, residents also live, work and enjoy life in and among its famous historic homes.

With that in mind, Charleston has created a Livability Court. Here, residents who wish to argue what seem like minor quality of life issues have their day. Owners of incessantly barking dogs, dilapidated yards and tour buses that stop in 'No Parking' zones are fined or sentenced, knowing a police officer has been assigned to follow up on their cases.

It's all part of what's called the "broken windows" approach to policing. It means that code violations and small infractions of the law encourage disorder, even crime, if left unaddressed.

What small problem area in your life might grow larger if left unaddressed?

Correct little by little. (Wisdom 12:2)

Help me embrace the discipline necessary for my own good, Lord.

Bonding Over Bagels

When was the last time you and your family sat down to enjoy a "family dinner?" If you're like most, the dinner hour is spent in activities other than sitting down and breaking bread together.

There are ways to reinstate a regular mealtime for your family, thus fostering closeness and strong ties. William Doherty, a marriage and family therapist, suggests "bonding over bagels," using breakfast to gather and communicate, however briefly.

Tips for encouraging communication, says Doherty, include aiming for the less hectic weekends; asking each family member to get to the breakfast table at a specific time and on time; and silencing phones, radios or televisions during the meal.

Nothing can replace or surpass the joy of real, meaningful connections and communication between you and another well-loved human being. Don't let the distractions of modern living interfere with that.

Martha welcomed Him into her home. She had a sister named Mary, who sat at the Lord's feet. (Luke 10:38-39)

Strengthen my family, Lord, so that we may truly learn to communicate and support one another.

Testing Faith, Teens Learn Who They Are

The teenage years are a critical time in developing faith. Here are a few tips for parents from Mark Oestreicher, an experienced youth pastor and author:

It's important for young people to evaluate their faith. Not doing so usually means they will either stagnate in their faith, going through life with a belief system that is not truly theirs, or step away from faith all together.

When kids ask questions about God it's okay for parents to admit they don't know the answer. Parent and teen working together to find answers and admitting struggles will do great things for a youngster's confidence in his or her faith.

Teens should be encouraged to get involved in programs which broaden their perspectives.

Teens are more likely to develop a long-lasting faith when they are supported in their spiritual efforts. As a parent or other concerned adult, reach out to the young people in your life.

Faith is the assurance of things hoped for, the conviction of things not seen. (Hebrews 11:1)

I pray that my faith in You, Lord, may serve as an example to others.

Three Short Minutes

There are 1,440 minutes in each day. If you are reading this page, you have chosen to devote three of those precious minutes to your inner life.

Those who write for *Three Minutes a Day* are constantly looking for messages of encouragement and hope. Our editor asks us to remember that variety is the spice of life. We read and we listen and we wrestle with words until we feel they help reveal the movement of God in the world.

We sift through magazine stories chronicling the generosity of others. We turn to our morning newspapers in search of nuggets of truth that might bring a smile or a tear or a nod of recognition from someone, somewhere looking for meaning and connection.

What brought you to this moment? What brought this book into your life? Pondering that simple journey itself ought to make you feel loved.

Love is strong as death. (Song of Solomon 8:6)

Thank you, Lord, for the many ways in which You touch our hearts each day.

Life's Hidden Gifts

One afternoon, Paul Schenk and his young son, Peter, planted bulbs in their garden. Halfway through the project, the tired father nearly said he'd be glad when they were finished. Then, memories of an afternoon with his own dad stopped him.

Schenk's father, Bill, once helped him with basement renovations. After working a while, he commented that he'd be glad when they were finished. His father replied that he and a coworker had once spent an entire day testing hundreds of parts for a NASA contract and he, too, had said that he'd be glad when they were finished. But his coworker responded, "Have you been testing transistors, Bill? I'm helping to send a man to the moon."

Bill Schenk then asked his son, "Have you been putting up corner molding? I've been spending the morning with my son."

Savor the little moments you share with loved ones. It is often then that life's true beauty is revealed.

From the greatness and beauty of created things comes a corresponding perception of their Creator. (Wisdom of Solomon 13:5)

I pray I don't get so distracted with life's pressures that I miss beautiful moments, Lord.

Music to Their Ears

Magee-Women's Hospital in Pittsburgh, Pennsylvania, is winning applause for its crooning doctor.

Breast-cancer surgeon Dr. Ronald Johnson belts out Bruce Springsteen and Kenny Rogers as he makes his rounds—even asking patients to join him. "Your doc is a human being and not a robot," says Johnson, whose singing puts patients at ease.

On New York's City Island, Elliott Glick, an art gallery owner, also uses music as part of his business day. His personal choices: classic vocal tunes from the 1940s and 1950s, and "anything by the Beatles." "There is a certain 'feel good' factor to that music, and that's part of bringing art to people," he explains. "As Duke Ellington said, 'If it sounds good, it is good.'"

No matter what work we do, if we do it with "a song in our heart," we'll surely bring a smile to another's face.

Be glad and shout for joy. (1 Peter 4:13)

I sing Your praises, Master, for You have surrounded us with the beauty of Your creation.

Hope on a Chain

When Cardinal François Xavier Nguyên Thuân, the former archbishop of Ho Chi Minh City (Saigon), died in 2002, many spoke of his legacy of love and hope.

Jailed for 13 years by the communist regime in his native Vietnam, he endured days of a brightly lit cell, followed by weeks of complete darkness. On the verge of madness, he convinced a young Christian boy to bring him some old calendars. On the backs of these he wrote messages of hope and love. These writings, smuggled out by that same boy, formed the book *The Road to Hope.*

While in prison, Cardinal Thuân also fashioned a cross and chain out of a small piece of wood and some electric wire. He wore that cross and chain every day of his life; it reminded him, he had said, that "only Christian love can change hearts; neither weapons, nor threats, nor the media can do so."

A legacy of love and hope–and a lesson on both as well.

Pray for those who persecute you.
(Matthew 5:44)

Give me the strength to accept sufferings as You did, Lord.

Going to the Head of the Parents' Class

"Not every teacher is a parent," says former U.S. Secretary of Education William J. Bennett, Ph.D., "but every parent is a teacher."

Here are some sure-fire ways to become an A+ parent.

1. Use the world as a classroom.

2. Eliminate limits. If your child wants to learn more about a subject, ask teachers to recommend books, videos, websites.

3. Teach your kids their way, visually, aurally or both. You will be more effective when helping with homework.

4. Read and continue your own education.

5. "Own" your children's education. Be involved with helping them.

Students and parents need to take personal responsibility for learning.

He went down with them...to Nazareth, and... increased in wisdom. (Luke 2:51,52)

Teach me Your ways, Father, that I may serve You this day.

"As You Wish"

William Goldman felt a special attachment to his novel, *The Princess Bride*. Years before, he had sold the novel's movie rights to a studio, but when the executive Goldman had dealt with was fired, all active projects at the studio were buried. That included *The Princess Bride*.

Despite the fact that Goldman was at a low point in his career as a screenwriter, he wanted to ensure that if his novel was ever made into a film, it was done right. So, Goldman bought back the film rights to *The Princess Bride*. This allowed the film to be made later, with Goldman's approval, by Rob Reiner. The result was a charming modern classic about, "fencing, fighting, revenge, giants, monsters, chases, escapes, true love [and] miracles," as the film's grandfather sums up.

The things we love are worth special attention. Even when it's difficult, remain loyal to yourself and the things important to you.

What is desirable in a person is loyalty. (Proverbs 19:22)

Lord, help us to strive for integrity.

From An Unlikely Beginning, Success

Wendy Cardella is the founder and director of NANA's house (Never Alone, Never Afraid), a haven for homeless Suffolk County, New York, families moving toward independence.

As a teen Cardella experimented with drugs and dropped out of high school just before graduation. Within four years a marriage had fallen apart, she had three children, no means of support and a foreclosed house.

But through community college classes, part-time jobs and work as a realtor she discovered her talent for helping poor families needing housing. And after five years working at a shelter she began NANA's House.

The talent for doing extraordinary good for the neediest is within each woman or man. It takes hard work and self-confidence to discover it.

Keep up your courage. (Acts 23:17)

Father God, I pray for the ability to use difficult times to grow and change.

Prizes and Ethics

The Kyoto Prizes were founded in 1984 to recognize achievements not covered by the Nobel Prize. Honorees are individuals and groups that benefit humanity by scientific, cultural, and spiritual development. Awards are given in three categories: advanced technology; basic science; arts and philosophy.

Past honorees have included scientists, composers, architects, linguists, artists and philosophers. Jane Goodall, the primatologist, was one of the laureates in 1990.

The founder, Kazuo Inamori, a Japanese industrialist said, "Now I'm thinking of expanding the third category of arts and philosophy, to add perhaps two more categories, so that more focus can be put on those aspects of human achievement."

Because material and technological goals appeared to replace doing "the right thing," Inamori wants to emphasize the importance of moral and ethical issues.

Everyone has a responsibility to meet life's moral obligations.

Do not think that I have come to abolish The Law or The Prophets; I have come not to abolish but to fulfill. (Matthew 5:17)

Lord Jesus, help us to live ethically.

Building Strong Children

There's nothing wrong with youngsters trying to increase their strength as long as they do it very safely.

Fitness coaches and pediatricians generally agree that children ages 12–14 can begin working with weights. However, cautions Greg Brittenham, a New York Knicks assistant coach in charge of training, "They should lift only under the supervision of a qualified trainer, and…the child's doctor (should be) aware of it."

Working out with weights can also improve bone structure and density, and help develop flexibility. But what about the youngster who trains with weights all summer but is disappointed when he doesn't see muscle development? Reassure him that the results of strength training over time is what counts.

Developing strength, spiritually, emotionally and physically is integral to growth. It takes time and there are no quick fixes. Encourage youngsters to grow, starting today.

Grow up in every way into...Christ...in love. (Ephesians 4:15, 16)

Guide parents to counsel their children well, Holy Spirit.

A Life Worth Imitating

Eleanor Roosevelt, a social activist and champion of many causes, continues to inspire new generations.

Her memory is kept alive in many ways, including the annual Girl's Leadership Workshop held at Val-Kill cottage, Mrs. Roosevelt's Dutchess County, New York, retreat. Here youngsters learn skills as they learn about Mrs. Roosevelt's life and times.

"Before coming here I'd heard of Eleanor Roosevelt," said one 16-year-old participant, "but I didn't know that she did so much for minorities and women."

Daniel A. Strasser, executive director of the Eleanor Roosevelt Center, said, "Most leadership courses stress being successful and making a lot of money but we want the girls to know that there is a side of their life where they can give to others."

Reach beyond immediate self-interest to concern for your greater, long-term good and for others' welfare.

Deborah, a prophetess, wife of Lappidoth... used to sit under the palm of Deborah...and the Israelites came up to her for judgment. (Judges 4:45)

May my personal legacy be admirable, Lord.

Seeing What Others Don't

Many scientists believe they are getting ever closer to vanquishing cancer. Dr. David Sidransky is one of them. His research philosophy is "think about the way things should be, then work backward and figure out how to make it happen."

Sidransky is a pioneer in testing to detect cancer at ever-earlier stages, thereby giving doctors better tools to spot tumors before symptoms appear. He focused on the DNA which is shed by tumors. For example, early tests have discovered 90 percent of bladder cancer tumors—an amazing rate.

Dr. Sidransky continues to follow the advice of his mentor, Dr. Bert Vogelstein, who told him to "think about things that are not so obvious."

Looking for the unseen makes every day an adventure for Sidransky. It can do the same for you.

Open your mind and heart to all God's wonders.

The sea...fled; Jordan turned back. The mountains skipped like rams, the hills like lambs...at the presence of the Lord. (Psalm 114:3-4,7)

Help us, Father, to see Your quiet handiwork in our lives. Help us to grow in appreciation for all Your gifts.

Cut the Clutter

If you are surrounded by clutter that you want to deal with once and for all, career counselor Barbara Sher offers tips that don't require getting organized or expending too much effort:

- Keep track of important things in a "go to jail/lose my home" box. Place only absolutely vital items in it; that way, when the time comes to address them, you'll know exactly where they are. Or, at the very least, you'll only have to search for the one box.

- Forget photo albums. Keep your unsorted photos in a box—not the previous box!—and store it within easy reach for spontaneous jags down memory lane.

- Instead of sporadic, all-day cleaning sessions, whenever you find yourself with a few minutes to spare, locate 10 things in the room that you can throw out. You will soon notice a difference in your living space.

Getting little things out of the way leaves more time for what really matters.

Do not judge by appearances. (John 7:24)

Lord, help us to differentiate between the important and the trivial in our lives.

The Death of Discussion

There is a troubling trend in Western society which has invaded our public dialogues, interactions with each other, and nearly everything we do as a society. We've become an argument culture.

Television talk shows, radio call-in programs, and public speeches all assume that to argue is the way to get your point across. To discuss an idea, set up a debate; to cover a news story, bring on spokespeople who have diametrically opposed views; to settle a dispute, call a lawyer.

When you're arguing, you generally aren't trying to understand what the other person is saying. You are focusing on what you'll say next.

If you do not begin a conversation with the assumption that there is "another side," you may miss the opportunity to learn something new.

Be sure your discussions aren't arguments.

Put away...bitterness and wrath and anger... and be kind to one another. (Ephesians 4:31,32)

I want my words to edify, not tear down. Help me in this, Jesus.

History Teaches Us Who We Are Today

The Matrix Marketing Research Company reports that nearly 60% of Americans have some interest in tracing their family history. In recent years, genealogy has become a significant pastime, with countless software packages and websites available to assist seekers in their quest to know their family's past.

Those in search of a more personal connection to their past are traveling far and wide, visiting cemeteries, libraries and courthouses in hopes of discovering information about their roots.

Sometimes seekers discover things they never knew, such as that a relative was wealthy, or died of a particular illness. Or, as was the case of one elderly woman, that she was of a different ethnic background than she was told. Sometimes these family history sleuths uncover previously unknown facts about their relatives and as a result learn a few things about themselves.

Studying your family's past can be instructive and fun. But your own todays and tomorrows are what really count.

Ascribe to the Lord the glory due His name. (1 Chronicles 16:29)

Savior, remind me that I am not alone.

Vocabulary, 2002

A witty friend sent an e-mail with a list of up-to-the-minute words. Enjoy them. And, smile!

Sitcoms–single income, two children, oppressive mortgage. That is, a former yuppie whose spouse stays home with the children.

Stress Puppy–someone who seems to thrive on being whiney and stressed out

Percussive Maintenance–the fine art of whacking an electronic device to get it to work again.

404–from the web error message "404 not found;" that is, a clueless person.

Mouse Potato–the on-line generation's couch potato

Ohnosecond–that micromillisecond in which you realize you've made a really big mistake.

Every generation has its own special words. But some words haven't changed: the language of love. Speak those unchanging words today

Each one heard them speaking in the native language of each. (Acts 2:6)

Amidst life's changes You are my rock, Abba. May I cling to You.

Looking Back, Moving Forward

At 19, Robin Smith's father, a Marine fighter pilot, was killed during a mission over Vietnam. For years, Robin resigned herself to the fact that her father had disappeared and she would never know what had really happened to him.

Then, as part of a documentary for a television newsmagazine, she visited the spot where her father had died. Before confronting her feelings, Vietnam was "a stone in my stomach," Smith said. But once she saw the site and, amazingly, her father's Naval Academy class ring was discovered, "the war no longer held me back," she said. For Smith, rather than being a stone, she sees the war as a touchstone, and feels she can begin to grow again.

While confronting painful memories is difficult, the only road to peace is through pain.

When a woman is in labor, she has pain...but when her child is born, she no longer remembers the anguish...So you have pain now; but I will see you again, and your hearts will rejoice. (John 16:21, 22)

Jesus, You suffered for us so that we may have eternal life. Thank You for showing me that peace can be achieved through hardship.

Compassionate Cop

When some people think of "cops" they think of guns and violence.

But Californian Joel Fay isn't anyone's notion of a typical police officer. With a Ph.D. in psychology, he is known as a friend of homeless people with mental illness.

"We talk about dreams, goals, and accomplishments. That really changes how you view a person," said Fay. He works with professionals in the probation, public defender and district attorney's offices to get homeless people needed help. It's not easy. Creativity, persistence and compassion are called for regularly.

Yet when his colleagues feel frustrated and hopeless, Fay says, "I try to be the carrier of hope that change is possible. I haven't always had that outlook – I think it comes from seeing so many 'hopeless' cases turn around."

Never give up. Hold on to hope.

Endurance produces character, and character produces hope. (Romans 5:4)

Encourage us, Jesus, to have a positive and hopeful view of the world.

It's a Special Day

Can you make *today* special? Here are just three suggestions:

Look for the good. Whether it's a beautiful sunset or a funny comic strip or a conversation with an old friend, seek out happy moments.

Be grateful: for your loved ones and family and their love; for your faith; your home or apartment; warm showers; comfy attractive clothing; plentiful food; your job and your loved ones' jobs; the weather, even if it is raining or snowing; your physical ability to do your work or the tasks at hand.

Give praise: for great service in a store or restaurant; to your loved ones for, of course, their love, but also for their talents, abilities, strengths, characteristics; to children, the elderly and infirm.

Life is bursting with joy, if only we know where to find it.

A joyful heart is life itself. (Sirach 30:22)

God, life is neither easy nor pleasant all the time. Still it is full of joy. Help me find and appreciate this hidden joy.

Giving Great Gifts

All through the year we wrestle with limited budgets and long gift lists for birthdays and other special occasions. Solutions exist.

Perhaps you're noted for your saffron chicken or paella or marble bundt cake. Compile its recipe and other favorites into a personal cookbook. Give the cookbook with some homemade goodies.

Purchase multiple copies of a one-year inspirational book. Send copies to distant friends with a note that during the year you'll be on the same page though you are far apart.

Give a family membership to a local museum or zoo. Include information about member-only benefits.

Give you children's teachers coupons to your local office supply store, coffee shop or book store.

Your recipients will appreciate your gifts and you'll be happy you made it more personal.

God loves a cheerful giver. (2 Corinthians 9:7)

Jesus, remind us that it is the thought—and thoughtfulness—that count, not the monetary value of our gifts.

Partners in Peace

Their names are Aisam-Ul-Haq Qureshi and Amir Hadad. In their eyes they are simply friends and tennis partners; to some people in some parts of the world they shouldn't be.

Qureshi, a Pakistani Muslim, and Hada, an Israeli Jew, first joined forces in 2002 to compete at Wimbledon, where they reached the final sixteen. As a result of their pairing, Qureshi was nearly banned from tennis by the Pakistan Sports Board, but he and Hadad kept playing.

Qureshi's response to the controversy? "I don't like to (mix) religion or politics into sports. You have to keep sport as a sport and just enjoy it." Hadad added "Aisam and I are friends first and Arabs or Jews second."

Qureshi and Hadad are proof positive that friendships can blossom at any time, among any and all peoples.

Be open to friendship.

A harvest of righteousness is sown in peace for those who make peace. (James 3:18)

Lord, help us to see all as brothers and sisters.

The True Test of Time

Quick, take this quiz:

- Name the five wealthiest people in the world
- Name 10 people who have won the Nobel or Pulitzer prizes.
- Name the last six best actor/actress Academy Award winners.

How did you do? If you're like most people, probably not that well. Now try this quiz:

- List teachers who aided your journey through school.
- Name three friends who have helped you through a difficult time.
- Name five people who have taught you something worthwhile or made you feel appreciated and special.

Easier, right? The people who truly make a difference in our lives are often not the subject of news broadcasts or newspaper articles. They are, however, the ones who make our lives worthwhile through their love and caring.

Return the favor.

Be kind to one another, tenderhearted. (Ephesians 4:32)

In the quiet moments of this day, I will find You, Father, and feel Your love.

Staying Open To New Experiences

When Linda Curia moved to Garden City, New York, from Staten Island, she didn't know what kind of people her new neighbors were. Nor did she know that her husband would die at the World Trade Center.

As new residents of the upscale town on Long Island, Linda and Larry Curia had wondered if their community might be unfriendly, or even snobby. But after Larry was killed, Linda learned about the warmth and kindness of her neighbors. Hearty meals. Home repairs. Companionship. Neighborly gifts helped Linda in her early days of grief and as she began raising two young children alone.

Said one neighbor, "We put our arms around her and said, 'We'll never desert you.'"

How ready are you to say that about a neighbor in need?

The merciful lend to their neighbor. (Sirach 29:1)

God, help us face all of the challenges of life.

The Sorrow of Tomorrow

Edgar Guest, known as "the poet of the people," wrote upwards of 11,000 poems before his death in 1959. "I take simple everyday things that happen to me and to a lot of other people," he said, "and I make simple rhymes out of them."

One poem which addresses the commonplace habit of good intentions that are never fulfilled begins:

"He was going to be all that a mortal should be/Tomorrow.

"No one should be kinder or braver than he Tomorrow…" and it concludes

"But the fact is he died and he faded from view, and all that he left here when living was through was a mountain of things he intended to do/Tomorrow."

When your tomorrows have turned into yesterdays, there may only be regret if you haven't made the most of your todays.

(God) has made everything suitable for its time. (Ecclesiastes 3:11)

Maker of Time and Eternity, help me use Your gift of time well.

Answered Prayers

Life was good, although hectic, for David and Merrily Rinehart, young parents of Katelyn and triplets, Clay, Jack and Sam.

But then doctors discovered Merrily had a brain tumor.

Immediately before her surgery–an operation that might leave her paralyzed or in a vegetative state–Merrily "kissed and hugged" her children, and then "talked, cried and prayed" with her husband.

"Although I didn't know it at the time," Merrily says, "people throughout our town–and across the country–were also praying for me. Word of my situation had spread, and I was on prayer lists from coast to coast."

Those prayers were answered. The Missouri mom returned home to her family. Surgery and radiation eradicated the tumor, and subsequent check-ups indicate it has not returned. The whole experience, Merrily says, "left me with a greater understanding of just how much we need to treasure every moment of life."

Bear one another's burdens. (Galatians 6:2)

I trust in Your goodness, Father, and believe in Your love.

Your Spiritual Life in Your Own Words

If you think about spiritual autobiographies, names like Augustine, Teresa of Avila and Thérèse of Lisieux come to mind. But psychologist Richard Patterson suggests that "each of us has a spiritual story worth telling–not so much for the benefit of others but for our own growth and enrichment."

Dr. Patterson, author of *Writing your Spiritual Autobiography,* says that your journal should be just between you and God. He suggests "humble honesty," about your doubts, struggles and actual beliefs, not what you think you ought to believe. Consider people–parents, teachers or influential authors–who have affected your faith. And do write about larger issues: your image of God, your experiences of prayer and of suffering.

In time, you may gain more knowledge and understanding than you might ever have imagined.

If while we were enemies, we were reconciled to God through the death of His Son, much more surely...will we be saved by His life. (Romans 5:10)

Blessed Trinity, grant me the wisdom and courage to learn about myself.

Words of Wisdom

Thousands of years ago a scribe or scribes or perhaps even "Solomon son of David, king of Israel," wrote the Bible's book of Proverbs. These aphorisms are always wise and often humorous.

The production of this often witty wisdom hasn't stopped. Here are some modern examples of such pithy words of wisdom:

- The best way to get even is to forget.
- To forgive is to set the prisoner free, and then discover the prisoner was you.
- Feed your faith and your doubts will starve to death.
- God wants spiritual fruit, not religious nuts.
- Too many people offer God prayers, with claw marks all over them.
- The tongue must be heavy, because so few people can hold it.
- A successful marriage isn't finding the right person–it's being the right person.

Genuine wisdom is always hard won but worth both the effort and the living out of it. Seek wisdom. Live it. Today.

Wisdom is radiant and unfading...easily discerned by those who love her and...seek her. (Wisdom of Solomon 6:12)

Give us the courage to seek wisdom, God.

Success and a Second Chance

When screenwriter Joss Whedon saw what they had done to his screenplay, he cried. "I really thought I'd never work again," he recalls of the experience. "It was that devastating."

In a classic tale of Hollywood disillusionment, Whedon had lost control of what he described as his "populist feminism" horror/comedy, *Buffy the Vampire Slayer*, and had seen it turned into a campy, badly-received farce. His strong female hero had been replaced with a ditzy cheerleader. The burgeoning screenwriter was crestfallen.

Yet several years later, Whedon regained control of *Buffy* and was able to launch it as a television series, returning the show to the original concept of his screenplay. The show has received popular, critical – and, surprisingly, even academic – acclaim, spawned a spin-off and has been nominated for several Emmys. Whedon, meanwhile, has become a successful television producer.

Second chances might be rare, but they do happen. Be sure to take full advantage of them.

Keep alert...be courageous, be strong.
(1 Corinthians 16:13)

Lord, help us see opportunity when we might otherwise overlook it.

Uncovering a Treasure

In 1864 a flag was presented to the Treasury Guard Regiment in Washington, D.C. It later showed up in parades honoring Civil War veterans.

The flag was then put in storage until Captain Henry Cobaugh eventually gave it to Edgar Yergason of Hartford, Conn. Yergason bequeathed it to his son, Robert. And in 1922, he donated it to the Connecticut Historical Society.

Seventy-six years later, the flag was discovered by Kelly Nolin, head of the society, as she was preparing a lecture on the Civil War. Retracing its history with expert help, Nolin showed that the flag had originally been borrowed from the United States Treasury to decorate the presidential box at the Ford Theatre the night President Abraham Lincoln was assassinated. Some accounts even say Lincoln grabbed the flag when he was shot.

History can teach so much. Be open to learning.

The memory of the righteous is a blessing. (Proverbs 10:7)

Show me how to treat all the world as sacred, Lord.

Back on Track

Julie Morgenstern, author of *Organizing from the Inside Out*, knows that many people who seem disorganized actually have other issues. Here are a few tips she offers to those who always find themselves taking on too many projects.

- Be alert for the idea "that if you turn down one chance…you'll never get another offer. This irrational belief leads to overextending yourself."

- "Gauge your attention span for each task." Morgenstern says that if you know you can only tolerate 20 minutes of bill-paying, you shouldn't spend an hour. Your time will be unproductive.

- Increase your value at work by saying, "No." Focus on your most substantial assignments. You will be in the best position to succeed.

We have many decisions to make each day. Take the time to give them the attention they deserve.

Clothe yourselves with compassion, kindness, humility, meekness and patience. (Colossians 3:12)

Lord, you are the Savior of the world, not me. Guide me in the choices I make every day.

People Who Ought to be Famous

In an issue about celebrities, editors at *Utne Reader* magazine decided to include hard working, talented people making a difference. These are a few of their "not-yet famous people who ought to be":

Octavia E. Butler, science fiction pioneer. Our "foremost African-American female science fiction writer...combines a down-to-earth social reality with other-worldly details."

Theo Colburn, senior scientist for the World Wildlife Fund. "Alerted the world to the threat of endocrine disrupters–synthetic chemicals that imitate or block hormones and are linked to a range of health problems" in her book *Our Stolen Future*.

Ernesto Cortes, Jr., Southwest regional director of the Industrial Areas Foundation. "His efforts have resulted in water and sewage treatment facilities for 400 Rio Grande Valley communities and 600 well-paying jobs for low-income people in San Antonio."

Whom would you nominate?

The farmer waits for the precious crop...being patient with it...you also must be patient. (James 5:7,8)

Thank you, Lord, for all the hard-working, not-yet famous people who are making a difference for the better.

A Super Man

In a documentary chronicling the recuperation of Christopher Reeve, who became a quadriplegic after breaking his neck in 1995, the actor is seen with his family, working with therapists, attending fund raisers and addressing legislators.

A pilot, sailor and equestrian, Reeve spoke about the challenge of supporting on-going spinal cord research. He also admitted he wished it were not his burden to bear.

In one of the most poignant scenes in the documentary, Reeve's 11-year-old son, Will, asks him if he knows where Northford, Connecticut, is. "No," answers Reeve, "but I'd be really interested in finding out."

It was a sincere and spontaneous response, speaking volumes about Reeve's priorities. Despite his situation, he is actively involved in parenting his children. How lucky they are to have each other.

Children need loving parents with all their abilities—and disabilities.

Honor your father, and do not forget the birth pangs of your mother. (Sirach 7:27)

Don't let me see the obstacles, Loving Creator. Help me live to my fullest potential.

In Tijuana, They Serve Smiles on Sunday

When Sonia Valdez arrives at the shanties near Tijuana, Mexico, residents run, limp and roll in in makeshift wheelchairs, lining up to receive free medical treatment.

The Orange County, California, nurse made her first trip to the area in 1989 with Dr. Tomio Hirota. After his death in 1998, she launched the nonprofit group Sonrisa (Spanish for "smile") in his memory.

On the second Sunday of every month, Valdez, doctors and volunteers drive down with donated equipment, vitamins and prescription drugs. Working from their cars, they treat infections, give checkups and thrill expectant mothers with the sound of their baby's heartbeat.

One woman, her foot pain cured, "gave me a hug," Valdez remembers. That hug and so many more from grateful patients keeps Valdez and the other volunteers smiling long after each trip ends.

Show your gratitude to those who help others.

There may come a time when recovery lies in the hands of physicians. (Sirach 38:13)

When my spirit is shattered, I seek Your healing love, Divine Physician.

Experiments and Fresh Thinking

What can chance breakthroughs in science teach us? Consider:

When a Raytheon engineer was walking through a room where a magnetron was being tested, the chocolate bar in his pocket began to melt. When the magnetron was pointed at an egg, it cooked so quickly it burst. Two years later, in 1947, Raytheon produced the first microwave oven.

The creation of high-speed cars introduced the need for higher-octane gasoline at an affordable price for the average consumer. Inventors were desperately seeking a solution. In the middle of their experiments the lab equipment of two Phillips Petroleum research chemists became clogged with a cloudy solid. The pair had discovered crystalline polypropylene, which with its cousin polyethylene, is the basis of today's plastic industry.

Learn to let go; to try the new. Stay open and flexible. You never know what you may discover!

As He walked by the Sea of Galilee He saw two brothers...And He said to them, "Follow Me." (Matthew 4:18,19)

I seek a fuller understanding of Your ways, Lord.

A World of Words

About 80 percent of the English language is said to be "foreign-born." In fact, the *Oxford English Dictionary* lists words from over 500 other languages–from Abnakei to Zuni–that are now used in English.

The languages from which English has borrowed most are Latin, French and German. *Posse,* familiar from so many Western films, comes surprisingly from Latin, as does the conjurors' word *abracadabra.* Many words from the French–*amateur, malaise* and *décor*–easily betray their origin, as do some German-based words–*blitz, lager* and *kitsch.*

There are also English words from other parts of Europe, as well as from Asia–the Chinese *ketchup* and *typhoon*–and from Africa–*banjo, tote* and *voodoo.*

A few words like *camcorder, guesstimate* and *sitcom* are American, arisen from popular culture and technology.

What's in a word? Could be the whole world.

In the beginning was the Word and the Word was with God, and the Word was God. (John 1:1)

I sing Your praises, Master, from the rising of the sun until the end of day.

Why Kids Love Fantasy Heroes

Parents, teachers and other observant adults know that children of a certain age are attracted to super heroes like Wonder Woman or the X-Men as well as other characters.

What's the appeal? According to psychologist Dr. Dan Acuff, children find these fantasy figures nurturing. A character like Barney the dinosaur nurtures; Blue the dog encourages the child's own caretaking skills.

Children also identify with these problem-solving characters because they have the super abilities children want. Fictional characters are entertaining. And, finally, while a child might not want to be Darth Vader, such a character shows a clear distinction between good and evil.

Help kids by talking about what makes a real hero: caring about others, making the world better, using God's gifts, respecting themselves.

Train children in the right way. (Proverbs 22:6)

Jesus, bless the little children.

Turning Discards into Dividends

According to antiques restorer turned builder Dan Phillips, "Ten percent of the average landfill is reusable building material." Taking that premise to heart, Phillips has spent the last six years helping working people buy a good home built with the "leftovers."

Phillips insists enough material is thrown away to build a house every week. But just because a house is being built with salvaged materials doesn't mean creativity and quality go out the window. The Huntsville, Texas, resident says, "Once you realize you can create stuff, it bleeds into every corner of your life." His wife, an arts teacher, even describes their life together as "a creative adventure."

Dan Phillips is fulfilling a long-held dream of helping the less fortunate in his own unique way. We all possess the power of creativity. Turning that creativity into positive results for others is high on the "doing good" chart. Don't be afraid to put yourself on the line and reap the rewards that giving brings.

A generous person has cause to rejoice. (Sirach 40:14)

Creator, may I be inspired to be creative and to give of myself.

A Retiring Approach

After serving in the Marines, Don McGehee made his living as a prison warden in Tennessee. Eventually he was director of probation and parole. But in retirement he has decided to make an impact at four elementary schools in Nashville, Tennessee.

McGehee, having spent his career helping to rehabilitate criminals, understands the importance of inspiring young people to make good choices. A gifted speaker, he routinely visits classrooms in four different schools to share cookies, time, and an interesting story or two incorporating character and morality.

McGehee has now established a small program called Project Altruism. He and a few friends fund it, giving students incentives to build records of good behavior. Winners use their prizes to support charities ranging from the Humane Society to local hospitals.

It's easy to fret about the younger generation. Do something to help them, instead.

Our hope for you is unshaken. (2 Corinthians 1:7)

Thank you, Lord, for your many blessings. Help me find ways to pass them on.

A Lifetime Believing and Writing

Not letting negative voices stop you can be difficult, but persistence often pays huge dividends. Take Eudora Welty, the acclaimed American writer, who died at 92.

Welty never stopped writing, even when critical acclaim didn't come. A Jackson, Mississippi, native, she lived and died in the same home she had occupied since high school, with the exception of a brief period spent in New York.

Enamored of books and writing, Welty's work remained unpublished until a small literary journal paid her $25 for a story. Even then Welty found herself pigeonholed with such other Southern writers as William Faulkner and Flannery O'Connor and dismissed as a regional author.

But Welty paid no mind. By the end of her life, she had won many prizes, including the Pulitzer.

Believe in yourself and value the talents God gave you.

Let us run with perseverance the race that is set before us, looking to Jesus the pioneer and perfector of our faith. (Hebrews 12:1)

Inspire and bless writers and editors, Lord of Sinai, Giver of Torah.

The Family Way

We see them all around us. Strong, loving, happy families who seem to be unfamiliar with the kind of chaos most of us experience on a daily basis.

Don't be fooled; everyone struggles. But Dr. Joyce Brothers provided some insight into the secrets of successful families in *Parade* magazine.

Among her ideas was that family must come first. "Strong families sacrifice to show support," Brothers says, pointing to the example of a father who turned down a luxury company vacation to attend his son's championship soccer game.

Brothers says strong families also treat each other well. "Positive strokes outnumber negative broadsides by a wide margin," she notes. Another non-negotiable is time. "Strong families do more than hope for time," says Brothers, "they insist on it. They set work boundaries and prioritize family fun."

Don't take your home life for granted. Do work at it.

I pray that...you may be strengthened in your inner being...and that Christ may dwell in your hearts through faith, as you are being rooted...in love. (Ephesians 3:16,17)

Help us cherish the precious family relationships with which you have blessed us, Lord.

"A Life Out There"

Far too many people know what it's like to have violence intrude on their lives. But, as with so many of life's painful moments, it's our response that makes all the difference.

When Horace Polite-Cobb witnessed the murder of a high school classmate in a pointless argument, the shock and grief propelled him into action. The honor student decided to join Youth Crime Watch of America (YCWA) which trained him in crime prevention and conflict resolution. After he helped initiate the program in his school, he assisted in resolving problems among students before they escalate.

"There's always a life out there that needs our help," said Horace Polite-Cobb. "That's why we have to stay with it, no matter what."

Decrying the world's suffering, including our own, will never improve anything as much as the simplest constructive action. For your sake, as well as for others, do something good, something right, something now.

Help the weak, be patient with all.
(1 Thessalonians 5:14)

Holy Lord, in times of confusion and loss, let me reach out to You and Your children to get and to give help.

Extra! Extra! Read All About My Great Kid!

While all parents have frustrating days with their children, most of the time mothers and fathers see their kids as wonderful gifts from God. Consider these creative ways to communicate that fact to children:

- Give your child an inexpensive framed certificate mentioning "20 things I like about you."

- On a Saturday morning surprise him or her by going out to breakfast–one-on-one.

- Have a T-shirt or mug made with your child's picture on it. Wear the shirt or take the mug to work–noting that you're advertising to others what a great kid you have!

- Place your hand on your child's head and pray for him or her aloud by name, saying, "Thank you, God, for such a wonderful gift." Then give your "gift" a hug.

Remember, a loving home atmosphere prepares kids for lives of hope and love.

Happy is everyone who fears the Lord. ...Your children will be like olive shoots around your table. (Psalm 128:1,3)

Father, help me to not only love my children, but also to let them know I do.

One of the Elite

After 13 years with the Los Angeles County Sheriff's Department, Sue Burakowski became the first female member of the elite Sheriff's Emergency Services Detail. The job's challenges are many, but none as difficult as qualifying for the unit. As her boss puts it, "Her desire is her strength."

Burakowski trained for a year to be certified as an expert mountaineer, paramedic and diver. "Work hard and never complain" became her motto. She has earned the respect of the men who are now her colleagues.

Reaching her goal has cost her personal time, but still she was able to foster parent Corey and David, the boys she plans to adopt.

She also dreams of inspiring girls to follow in her footsteps. "I want to have some little girl meet me at a job fair and say, 'I want to do this someday.'"

Dream big and work hard to achieve a goal. The feeling of self-satisfaction to be gained is enormous.

Human success is in the hand of the Lord. (Sirach 10:5)

Remind me that dreams and hard work are the key, Merciful Savior.

Something Out of Nothing

Johnny B. Thomas was only a boy when his hometown of Glendora, Mississippi, was literally wiped out. Fires decimated the town's business district, extinguishing the community's economy and job prospects.

Over the years, most of the residents moved away. A handful remained and they elected Thomas mayor. Although the town remained desolate with bleak prospects and little growth, Thomas dove into his role as community leader with zeal. "Somehow, I've been hooked on bringing the town back," he says.

Since he took office almost two decades ago, his vision, creativity and perseverance have helped revive the town. New industries are budding along with improved job prospects for many.

Your community is only as good as you help make it. It needs your input to survive.

Blessed are those who hunger and thirst for righteousness, for they will be filled. (Matthew 5:6)

Jesus, You illustrated the importance of community among Your own apostles. I pray I can become a better citizen of my own community.

E-mail–Clear and Civil

"The ideal breeding ground for rudeness," is how Patricia T. O'Conner and Stewart Kellerman, authors of *You Send Me,* see e-mail.

Writing in *The New York Times Magazine,* they describe an "ideal of e-mail perfection." Each message:

- is in clear, plain, understandable English
- uses words like, "please," "sorry," and "thanks"
- gets to the point quickly
- is discreet and protects the privacy of all
- says what a reply concerns, instead of just "yes" or "no"
- has a useful subject line
- capitalizes properly for easier reading
- avoids technical and shorthand terms
- has been reread with care

In other words, write–and e-mail–to others as you would have them write–and e-mail–to you.

Show every courtesy. (Titus 3:2)

Holy Spirit, encourage us to be courteous in all our words and actions.

Heavenly Flowers – Literally!

During the Middle Ages, gardeners found reminders of Mary, the mother of Jesus, in the flowers and herbs around them.

Marigolds and Madonna Lilies are named after her, and many others have legends associated with her. These include the Columbine, or Our Lady's Shoes, which were said to have sprung up in Mary's footsteps, and the Lily of the Valley, or Mary's Tears, which grew at the foot of Jesus' cross where Mary wept.

Mary's Gardens, with some of the flowers and herbs that bear legends of her life can be created in a flowerpot or in your backyard. Start with a little research at the library or on the Web.

Let the beauty of the flowers remind you of Mary's strength of character, fidelity to her faith and hard life in an occupied land, as well as the simple joys of her life as the wife of Joseph the carpenter and the mother and disciple of her Son, Jesus.

A capable wife...is far more precious than jewels. ...Her children rise up and call her happy; her husband too. (Proverbs 31:10,28)

Jesus, protect all women in their struggles, hardships and challenges, as well as in their joys.

A Simple Solution

"When my children were young, we took long walks along the creek by our house, or played on the floor. Somehow I'd lost much of that intimacy," T. Suzanne Eller writes.

Seeing her reflection in a store mirror one day caught Eller by surprise. "As I stared into the eyes of this weary stranger," she admitted, "I knew my life had to change."

For Eller, that meant examining the gap between her reality and her priorities, which she listed as God, family, health, ministry and work.

"Simplify, simplify, simplify," has become her new mantra. "If I keep saying it to myself, then one day it just might be second nature," she asserts.

Most of us come to crossroads moments when it's time to reevaluate our approach to life. Have the courage to examine your own way of living.

Have you examined your priorities? ...simplified your life?

Be on your guard against all kinds of greed; for one's life does not consist in the abundance of possessions. (Luke 12:15)

Remind me, O Lord, that You have already saved the world.

A Hunger-Free Society

Actor Jeff Bridges was stunned. It was the late 70s. At a lecture he attended on world hunger, he learned that the deadly problem could exist even in prosperous times, when money to buy food was so plentiful.

Bridges co-founded the End Hunger Network in 1983 to galvanize volunteers, educate politicians, and generate more than $60 million to help aid the hungry.

Now, Bridges focuses his efforts on the more than 33 million Americans, many of whom are children, who are hungry. He writes letters to elected officials, tapes public service announcements and even co-produced the 1996 film, *Hidden in America,* about a hungry family's struggle to survive.

Jeff Bridges says ending hunger must be a priority for others, too. "People think charity can handle this. It can't. Food banks and hunger groups are doing a great job, but they can't do it alone. It's bigger than that."

What are you doing to fight hunger?

Give some of your food to the hungry. (Tobit 4:6)

Spirit, guide me to generosity.

Still at War

When, during the Civil War, Confederate General Robert E. Lee led a surprise attack against the Union Army at Chancellorsville, thirty thousand soldiers died, including General Thomas Jonathan (Stonewall) Jackson.

Today the battlefield is within commuting distance of Washington, DC. Developers want to use the part of the land adjacent to the main battlefield for a family-friendly community which, they say, would respect the land's history. They are willing to set aside 34 acres honoring those who fought.

Preservationists fear that the site will eventually come to the same fate as one in Franklin, Tennessee where an historic marker is sandwiched between two pizza parlors. A similar fate has met other sites around the U.S.

We need to balance today's needs with our respect for and interest in the past. It is important to remember the past lest we repeat the same mistakes time and time again.

Let us now sing the praises of...our ancestors... who made a name for themselves by their valor. (Sirach 44:1,3)

Holy Spirit, shower us with wisdom and patience, even when circumstances seem hopeless.

Keep Moving

Veralyne Fenty has a motto she lives by. "Depression can't hit a moving target, so I keep moving," says the 68-year-old, who was named 2002 Volunteer of the Year for Colorado.

She didn't always feel that way. When Fenty lost her sight in a 1975 car accident, she almost took her own life.

"I thought it was the end of the world," she says in looking back at the time she woke up blind. But, "I ended up in a psych ward and 18 months later I came out with a smile." Ever since, she has given of herself and inspired others. As a counselor at senior center vision program, Fenty helps others cope with blindness.

Veralyne Fenty is the personification of never giving up hope and a can-do attitude. Volunteering helps her "to practice what I preach," and it can do the same for any of us.

Reach out today and give of your time and yourself.

Do not neglect to do good. (Hebrews 13:16)

May I see a need and help fill it, Great Giver.

A Dream for Weeksville

The Society for the Preservation of Weeksville knows how important dreams are. Located in the Bedford-Stuyvesant section of Brooklyn, Weeksville is the remains of one of the earliest communities of freed slaves. It is also thought to have been a stop on the Underground Railroad. The members of the society have spent the last 30 years working towards restoring the community and educating outsiders on its rich history.

Founded in 1838 by James Weeks, a longshoreman who is thought to have been a slave himself, the area soon attracted former slaves, since New York had outlawed slavery in 1832.

Now, the little clapboard cottages need to be restored. Joan Maynard, the group's retired executive director says, "Everyone should know what happened here. These houses can't speak for themselves."

Persistence is more powerful than any circumstance that gets in the way of a dream.

Be persistent. (2 Timothy 4:2)

Lord, teach us patience and endurance when faced with adversity.

A Marriage of Service

David and Suzanne Kammer met while serving as community organizers in Detroit.

David went on to law school and today represents employees who have been discriminated against or mistreated by their employers. It doesn't bring in lots of money–but it does make a difference in people's lives.

Making a difference for others is important to this Cincinnati couple. These days a stay-at-home mom, Suzanne hopes to pass that vision on to their three children. David does too. "I tell them what Jesus wants us to do is to help each other," he explains.

"I often ask God what He is going to do about this or that," Suzanne says. "But then I ask, what am I going to do about it. I know I can't reach the goal of feeding the whole world, but I'll do what I can."

All we can do is all we can.

When you give alms, do...so...in secret; and your Father who sees in secret will reward you. (Matthew 6:3,4)

This day, Father, help me to bring Your light to one person in darkness; Your love to one person in pain.

Prom Night? What's That?

Prom night is important for many teenagers in U.S. high schools. But countless immigrant parents don't know what a prom is and don't want their kids going, though the youngsters are anxious to fit in.

"If I were to explain to my parents what the prom is, I'm sure their reactions would be 'Huh?'," said Zhi-De Deng. "Parties past midnight aren't common in their experience."

Some immigrant youngsters go with a group of friends rather than an individual date. "It's not going to be a prom like in the movies," said Russian-born Svetlana Bezinyan. "But it's nice."

Nowrin Khanam, from Bangladesh, couldn't persuade her mother to grant permission for the prom. "She said, 'Next time,' but how is there going to be a next time?"

Loving parents, native-born and immigrant, have different experiences and expectations from their children. Teens and their parents need to negotiate a middle path.

"Child, why have You treated us like this? Look, Your father and I have been searching for You"...He said to them, "Why were you searching for Me? Did you not know that I must be in My Father's house?" (Luke 2:48,49)

As we deal with life's challenges, Lord, grant us patience, wisdom and understanding.

Treat Yourself Well

Many people work long hours, hold two jobs, rush from meeting to meeting; care for children, spouses, parents, employers, colleagues and neighbors. What they don't do often enough is care for themselves.

Woman's Day magazine asked its readers how they treated themselves to a little luxury in the midst of hectic lives.

Gail Albiston goes to lunch, dinner or a movie with her friends at least once a month. No husband or kids this time.

Rosalie Savage lies in a "hammock with a magazine, pillow and throw" relaxed by wind chimes and rustling trees.

Lora Sobolow spends a few hours on Saturday sipping tea and reading cookbooks in her bookstore's cafe.

Lainie Brubacher spends time with her pets.

Janet Minnich feels good giving someone a smile and seeing them return it.

Nurturing yourself renews your energy so you can help yourself and others.

You shall love...your neighbor as yourself. (Luke 10:27)

Jesus, show me how to better care for myself and others.

Myths about Leadership

Countless pages have been written about the qualities of a leader, but, at the same time, myths have arisen. Franklin Ashby and Arthur Pell, authors of *Embracing Excellence,* have debunked some common, but incorrect, notions.

For example, many people say that good leaders are poor followers. In reality, because they value and support teamwork, good leaders start as loyal followers.

Another myth is that good leaders are born that way. While it may apply to some, most leaders develop skill by confronting life's challenges. And while many believe that leaders must have high IQs, the range of intelligence is actually broad, especially since maturity and emotional well-being are equally significant.

Most importantly, good leaders understand that leadership itself is an opportunity for service.

Love is patient...not envious or boastful or arrogant or rude. ...it is not irritable or resentful... but rejoices in the truth. (1 Corinthians 13:4-5, 6)

Holy God, lead me in all I do, so that wherever I go, I seek Your will; whatever I do, I accomplish Your will.

Seeing-Eye Horse

Cuddles is a real cutie. The two-year-old can find her way around Atlanta's subway system and airport, as well as the streets of Manhattan. Two-feet tall and 55 pounds, Cuddles is a full-grown miniature horse; the first guide horse for the blind in the United States.

Some "neigh"-sayers might say that horses spook easily and might bolt in a crowd. Janet Burleson, founder of the nonprofit Guide Horse Foundation that trained Cuddles, disagrees. "During the eight-month training session, we teach horses to accept the normal things in human life, like pedestrians and cars," she explains. As proof, Burleson says, "Just look at police horses."

The demand for the seeing-eye horses is growing. Presently 80 people are on the waiting list, Burleson notes. Cuddles lives with her owner in Maine—and yes, she is housebroken.

What can you do to make life less challenging for the blind and those with impaired sight?

You shall not revile the deaf or put a stumbling block before the blind...I am the Lord. (Leviticus 19:14)

Show me the way, Master, that I may lead others to You.

Mixed Blessing

There are times when an action which is good for one group of people is resented by others.

In 1913, New York City needed a reliable supply of clean water and found it in upstate Ulster County. The Esopus Creek was dammed to create the Ashokan Reservoir.

Four Catskills hamlets were flooded; eight others, moved. Thousands of people had to relocate, after their houses, churches, schools, shops and sawmills had been cleared or moved. Even graves were disinterred.

Despite the disruption and the bitterness about a big city intruding on small towns, many residents of the Esopus Valley came to appreciate the beauty and benefits of the Ashokan Reservoir. Said one man, "the land will be forever wild and pure and gorgeous."

In the summer of 2002, New York City finally commemorated the sacrifices made by Ulster County residents with outdoor exhibitions in towns along the Hudson River.

When others make sacrifices, we need to return gratitude.

Give thanks in all circumstances.
(1 Thessalonians 5:18)

May we both appreciate our blessings, Lord, and the sacrifices made to ensure them.

Tips for Making the Grade

When it comes to helpful tips on children achieving success in school, few have better insight than principals. School heads from across the country participated in *Family Circle's* annual Principal's Hotline, fielding calls on issues that matter to parents. Here are just a few of their nuggets of wisdom:

- Be your child's student. Ask for a summary of a book he or she has read.
- Attend school events like PTA, plays, games.
- Suggest attacking hard homework tasks first.
- Encourage writing.
- Celebrate your child's nonacademic talents– music, drama, art, sports.
- Share your job, hobby or talent with your child's class.
- Partner with teachers to provide a positive view of school for your child.
- Review your child's progress at year's end. Children love hearing praise.

Listen to your children, and guide them well and lovingly.

He went down with them...to Nazareth, and was obedient to them. ...And Jesus increased in wisdom. (Luke 2:51,52)

Help me to be the best parent I can be, Father of all.

Before You Criticize

Though Aesop, teller of wonderful fables is supposed to have lived around 600 B.C. in Greece, many of his tales, such as "The Boy Who Cried Wolf," "The Fox and the Grapes" and "Androcles and the Lion" are still very well known.

But here's a useful one for those of us with a tendency to criticize to keep in mind:

A boy bathing in a river was in danger of being drowned. He called out to a passing traveler for help, but instead of holding out a helping hand, the man stood by unconcernedly, and scolded the boy for his imprudence.

"Oh, sir!" cried the youth, "pray help me now and scold me afterwards."

Aesop's moral: "Counsel without help is useless."

The fact is, a helping hand will always do more good than criticism—even if the criticism is accurate. Just ask yourself what you would want next time you're drowning in trouble.

Do not find fault before you investigate, examine first, and then criticize. (Sirach 11:7)

Jesus, You always stretch out Your hand in help and friendship. Please show me how to imitate You.

The Art of Forgiveness

In 1966 Air Force captain Pete Peterson was shot down over North Vietnam, and spent six and a half years as a prisoner of war.

For years, Peterson struggled with his feelings about his imprisonment. Despite his belief in forgiveness, he harbored grudges and experienced feelings of hatred.

However, the first time he returned to the village where he had been shot down, he was astounded by the villagers' reception. They greeted him with cheers and gifts. Peterson even met two of his three captors. They hugged him as they said "we saved you, and you saved us." The trio discussed how any one could have killed the other but that they had chosen not to and had managed to survive.

More than benefiting others, forgiveness releases us from destructive emotions and allow us to see a situation in a new perspective.

Be kind to one another, tenderhearted, forgiving one another, as God in Christ has forgiven you. (Ephesians 4:32)

Jesus, Your forgiveness is unconditional. Help me imitate it and truly forgive those who hurt me.

The Gift of Our Own Experience

Watching her friends constantly fight with their parents, 17-year-old Journey Henkart came to appreciate her open and honest relationship with her mom, Andrea, a counselor to teens and pre-teens.

Together they used what they had learned to co-write "Cool Communications: A Mother and Daughter Reveal the Keys to Mutual Understanding Between Parents and Kids." They are now leading mother-daughter workshops around the country.

They advise parents to acknowledge differences, to be good examples–and to choose "battles" wisely. And they urge young people to "appreciate and cooperate with your parents–and believe in yourself."

We sometimes don't realize know valuable our own life experiences are. But when we reach out to help others, we often find gold in our own memories.

Children ought not to lay up for their parents, but parents for their children.
(2 Corinthians 12:14)

Jesus, guide me daily.

Nature Nurtures

"In times of heartache and of fear, it has always been trees, birds, a stream that have sustained me, given me courage, and hinted at ways to continue on," writes Lisa Fugard.

Most of us will never know the quiet harmony found gliding through water in a kayak. Few of us will have the same kind of true awakening Fugard once experienced in a kayak after an emotionally difficult time in her life.

Coming upon a foraging raccoon, she watched it skitter into a tangle of roots. "I felt as though I were seeing water, tree bark, a raccoon for the first time and I was astounded at how beautiful it all was," she wrote.

Try not to discount the power of nature. A simple outdoor walk can refresh and renew sagging spirits in ways unlike any other tonic.

Wisdom praises herself...like rosebushes in Jericho; like a fair olive tree...and like a plane tree beside water I grew tall. Like cassia and camel's thorn...and...myrrh I spread my fragrance. (Sirach 24:1, 14, 15)

Thank You, Creator, for bounteous, beautiful life which reflects You, Your bounty and beauty!

Educating Youngsters About Steroids

When former major league baseball star Ken Caminiti admitted that he had used steroids to enhance his performance on the field, he also said he believed a large number of other big leaguers took them as well.

It was a clarion call to parents. The availability and attraction of steroids places the burden on parents to educate their children about how harmful the drugs are. Kids want to be like their favorite athletes, and they might think that if steroids helped those athletes succeed, then the same drugs might propel them along the same path.

Research indicates that more than 40 percent of high school seniors claimed steroids were easy to obtain. Parents must alert their kids to the documented side effects of steroids–drastic mood swings, depression, an enlarged heart, acne, premature baldness.

Parents must be on the front lines with positive messages educating youngsters. Deliver that anti-steroids message today.

The Lord...protects those who take refuge in Him. (Nahum 1:7)

Spirit of Wisdom, guide parents as they try to guide their children.

Can One Song Make a Difference?

Can one song make a difference? Many would answer with a resounding yes.

Throughout the ages music and songs have had an impact on our feelings, moods and behavior. Consider the example of a song called by some the "ultimate American protest song."

The tune we know as "We Shall Overcome" has been sung by a variety of groups championing such causes as civil rights, workers' rights and human rights.

"Some of the best protest songs are acts of reaffirmation," said Pete Seeger, noted folk singer, "like another sunrise or another kiss. It's well known that in periods of crisis, people want to sing together, to join hands and sing slow, serious songs that they all know."

Seeger adds, "It's important to make a noise. It's a way of saying, 'Yes, we are all here'."

Strive for justice, mercy and peace in your life.

Will not God grant justice to His chosen ones who cry to Him? (Luke 18:7)

Almighty Father, may we seek justice for all Your children.

A Big Difference for the Smallest Reasons

One evening in May 1996, as Debi Faris stood in the kitchen of her California home preparing dinner, she heard a news story about a newborn boy who had been found in a duffel bag along a freeway. "It just stopped me," Faris recalls. "Who knew this baby? Who would bury it? What was the mother thinking?"

After talking with her husband and children, Faris sought and got permission to bury the child. In the years since, Faris has repeated the sad ritual many times over–lovingly burying these infants in the Garden of Angels, a small cemetery east of Los Angeles.

Faris is also hoping to make a difference for other newborns, as she pushes for awareness of California's Safe Haven law which allows women to safely abandon their newborn child without prosecution.

"Secrets kill," Faris says. "I know, because I've buried 54 of them. But I also know that one person can make a difference."

Just as the Father has life in Himself, so He has granted the Son also to have life in Himself. (John 5:26)

Father, hear my cry for peace.

Everyday Greatness

In 1936, Briton Beryl Markham became the first person to fly solo from London to New York, nonstop.

Before her record-breaking transatlantic flight, Markham had made her living for several years as a bush pilot in Kenya, delivering supplies, passengers and mail to remote regions.

She once said, "If a man has any greatness in him, it comes to light, not in one flamboyant hour, but in the ledger of his daily work."

The daily, often mundane aspects of life rarely make us feel "great." Few can be a lifeline to the people of Kenya as was Markham. But we can be a lifeline to someone in our daily lives; strangers and friends.

"Greatness" doesn't come in one flash of glory but in the everyday thoughtful gestures and consideration we give our neighbors.

Whoever pursues righteousness and kindness will find life and honor. (Proverbs 21:21)

Lord, help us to see the greatness in helping one another.

The Work Continues

The Hawaiian Islands conjure up visions of sand, sun, fun, even paradise. But not too long ago, people would have thought "leper colony."

More than 100 years ago, Rev. Damien DeVeuster, a Belgian missionary to Hawaii, ministered to people with leprosy or Hansen's Disease. At that time there was neither prevention nor treatment, only confinement on the isolated Kaluapapa peninsula of Molokai.

Although Hansen's Disease is now treatable, Rev. DeVeuster's work continues. Three Franciscan nuns care for the physical, emotional and spiritual needs of the remaining patients.

When the need for the specialized medical facility ceases—medicines allow people with Hansen's disease to live at home—it will become an historic park, a monument to our "ability to conquer...not only leprosy but the stigma and rejection" that accompanied it.

Fighting stigma is a never-ending cause.

Ten lepers approached Him..."Jesus, Master, have mercy on us!" ...He said..."show yourselves to the priests." And as they went, they were made clean. (Luke 17:12, 13, 14, 15)

May I continue to struggle for what's right, Jesus.

Appreciating Our Differences

In the midst of diversity, finding common ground is a not impossible. Ask Erin Moriarty, a gardener whose days are spent at the fruit and vegetable stands of one of New York's most ethnically diverse neighborhoods.

The Queens Botanical Garden supports Ms. Moriarty's research into the food preferences of immigrants from such areas as China, Korea, India, Afghanistan and South America. They include favorites such as grass jelly drink, black sweet rice in banana leaves with coconut milk and salty dried yogurt balls.

Each of these is to some foreign, or even distasteful. People are always emphasizing the differences between cultures," said Ms. Moriarty, "but when you look at what we eat, you will see that there are a lot of the same basic foods, just prepared differently."

Can peoples whose native dishes look, taste and smell different get along? Can peoples who look and sound so different get along? Our humanity links us.

God created humankind...in the image of God... male and female He created them. (Genesis 1:27)

Remind us, Jesus, that we are members of one family, the human family.

The Spirit of Dunkirk

Albert Barnes was just 14 years old when he took part in Operation Dynamo, the 1940 "Miracle of Dunkirk." Civilians used fishing boats, yachts, any vessels they could get to help evacuate the British forces pinned down by the German army on the English Channel beaches near the French village of Dunkirk.

Sixty years later, Barnes recalled the thousands of soldiers trapped on the beach. "I was very frightened, terrified in fact," he said, "because there were German dive-bombers all around us. But we just got on with the job."

The "Spirit of Dunkirk" is not just a bit of history. Albert Barnes might tell you that the spirit lives on today in people who, no matter the circumstance, simply "got on with the job" of helping others.

That spirit of doing all we can to help others exists within each if us–if we only choose to make use of it.

Take courage; I have conquered. (John 16:33)

Father, guide us as we get on with job of helping all Your children, our brothers and sisters, in need.

Healing Presence

Janet Stookey, an operating room nurse in Alaska, uses her annual vacations to volunteer in countries where good medical care is rare.

"I felt a responsibility to help needy people since I was born and trained in the U.S.," Stookey said. "We're so prosperous, and just a little of what we have goes so far in other places."

Operation Blessing International seeks to show God's love by providing health care as well as food, clothes and shelter to impoverished Third World residents.

It's rewarding work.

"Once in Mexico, my team gave a nearly blind boy his first pair of glasses," said Stookey. "You couldn't wipe the grin off his face. He kept walking to the window to see everything outside."

How wonderful to enjoy abundance and to want to share it.

The yoke of their burden, and the bar across their shoulders, the rod of their oppressor You have broken. (Isaiah 9:4)

Give me the vision, Father, to see suffering and relieve it.

Up, Up and Away!

David Michel of Texas was having serious difficulty getting a particular project off the ground for his health care consulting firm. His wife suggested, "Maybe you should think about doing something else."

David fought this idea over the next few months. When his work required travel, he'd fight the pangs of loneliness and of missing his wife and child by making up stories to tell his young son.

Pretty soon, his nagging desire to follow his calling got the best of him–literally. As he tucked his son into bed one night, he realized the stories he made up and told his son each night might have mass appeal. The result: David became the creator of "Jay Jay the Jet Plane." First a video and then a television series for children, it became a huge success.

Following your heart often leads to greater success than one ever imagined. What are you most passionate about?

Listen and understand. (Matthew 15:10)

Jesus, I pray that I will discover my true calling in life so that I may do Your will.

Singing Hearts

Karen Speake cleaned teeth for 20 years. Today she works full time designing and painting murals. "My spirits are lifted to the skies," she says.

Becky Trowbridge left her job as an environmental engineer after 12 years to become a personal chef. "I find so much joy in leaving a client's home with the kitchen spotless, the freezer full with the next week's meals, and tonight's dinner in the oven," she observes.

History teacher Posy Lough left the classroom to produce the Posy Collection, gifts sold mainly through museum stores.

Each of these women found the courage to pursue her dreams. Each listened to her desires, evaluated her skills, and found a better way to use her talents. In doing so, each found true fulfillment.

What can you do, today, to move closer to fulfillment?

Wisdom is...easily discerned by those who love her...who seek her. She hastens to make herself known to those who desire her. (Wisdom of Solomon 6:12-13)

Holy Spirit, enlighten me as I strive to be my true self.

For Your Consideration

Eduardo Galeano, writing in *Upside Down*, penned his thoughts on ideas that would improve the world. Here are a few for your consideration:

- People shall work for a living instead of living for work.
- Politicians shall not believe that the poor love to eat promises.
- The world shall wage war not on the poor but rather on poverty, and the arms industry shall declare bankruptcy.
- You shall love nature to which you belong.
- In our bungling, messy world, every night shall be lived as it if were the last and every day as if it were the first.

We all need reminders that the challenge to live in right relationships, to live ethically, with God, our self, and others is ever ancient, ever new. How do you want the world to change? How are you going to make it happen—even in a small way—today?

Take up the challenge.

What does the Lord require of you but to do justice, and to love kindness, and to walk humbly with your God. (Micah 6:8)

Holy God, Author of Sinai's Commandments, guide our relationships—with You, with our very selves, with others.

A Match Made In Heaven

There are a lot of people interested in dating and finding a mate who insist on including their religious values in the mix.

"If I'm dating someone who doesn't understand my religious perspective, it's not going to work," said a 34-year-old Lutheran woman. He doesn't have to share her same beliefs, but "I want him to ask questions, not argue with me or dismiss my religion."

Another woman is happy now to be dating a man who, while he's not religious, does share her values of empathy and service to others. "Most important, he respects my spirituality. He even attends services with me from time to time."

Jane waits until the second or third date before mentioning her religious side. "I don't want to frighten someone into thinking that I'm out to convert him. Besides, I have to find out if I like the person before I trust him with my feelings about my faith."

You're more likely to make a good match with someone who shares your values.

Let them marry whom they think best. (Numbers 36:6)

Help us, Jesus, to build relationships on solid foundations.

Mutual Support in a Painful Time

The Roman Catholic Church in the United States has been facing scandal caused by allegations and admissions of pedophilia, and subsequent cover-up, by clergy and hierarchy. Many lay Catholics have been trying to come to grips with the situation. In Lexington, Kentucky, some got together to talk and pray.

"We wanted to bring the people together to provide prayerful support for each other," said Ginny Ramsey. The Lexington group shared the Eucharist at a Mass and then enjoyed a potluck supper before beginning their discussion and prayer.

In reaching out to each other in prayer and reflection, they found themselves providing other distressed Roman Catholics with a way through the crisis. "We plunged into a grief process that we never expected, and to get through it, we needed each other," says Ramsey. Another participant, Kabby Akers, adds: "It gave me an opportunity to do something concrete instead of just feeling bad."

In difficult times, find support in discussion and prayer.

Pray without ceasing. (1 Thessalonians 5:17)

I lift my voice in prayer, hear my cries and answer me, Father.

Patriotism in Today's World

What is patriotism? Patriotism can mean being willing to die for one's country.

But, in the United States, it also means ensuring that the Bill of Rights, the Declaration of Independence and the Constitution apply to all. As historian Norman Podhoretz has said, "if you don't know and appreciate those documents, you don't know what it means to be an American."

Sadly, there have been times when patriotism has been an excuse to abridge the rights of others rather than an encouragement to seek "liberty and justice for all." But that's not why our Founding Fathers dissolved the allegiance of 13 colonies to King George III. They did it so that what became the United States of America would be, as Lincoln later said, liberty's "last best hope."

A final thought: Patriotism, as Adlai Stevenson said, does not consist of "short, frenzied outbursts of emotion, but the tranquil and steady dedication of a lifetime."

You...repented and did what was right in My sight by proclaiming liberty to one another. (Jeremiah 34:15)

Author of our Liberty, give us that courage which you gave to the founders of the United States.

Picture Perfect!

The Harvard Museum of Natural History exhibited perfect flowers that were clearly crowd pleasers. Visitors oohed and aahed at seeing the carnivorous Mayan pitcher plant, the water lilies, the fleur-de-lis iris and others. The perfect flowers were beautiful but they weren't real.

In the 19th century a father and son team, Leopold and Rudolf Blaschka, turned their skill at making glass floral jewelry to making realistic glass flowers for study.

So perfect is a flower's imperfection that it takes awhile for today's museum goers to realize what they're observing is glass and not flowers, complete with all the bent leaves, missing petals and dirt covered roots that nature itself provides.

The glass botanical specimens are sturdy. But if they do break the illusion is also shattered because a broken milkweed, for example, doesn't ooze sticky sap.

We may be attracted by perfection and wish we didn't have our human foibles. But "only human" isn't bad.

If you wish to enter into life, keep the Commandments. (Matthew 19:17)

God, help us to appreciate one another, warts and all.

Just One of the Guys

How do you define success?

Mary Wells Lawrence could certainly meet most definitions. Head of the advertising giant Wells Rich Greene, Lawrence was the first female CEO of a company traded on the New York Stock Exchange.

Breaking through both corporate and discriminatory barriers in a male-dominated industry in the 1970's didn't come without a high cost. "It takes a tremendous amount of aggression and single-mindedness to get to the top of a company," she says. "You work 46-hour days. You put in all your energy. And everything else is an accessory to your life."

Mary Wells Lawrence has undoubtedly helped open doors for women in business. But the good news is that each of us can work for justice, in ways big and small. One doesn't have to be a CEO. Courage—and a desire to look out for the other guy—is all that's needed.

Be brave. (Sirach 19:10)

Lord, I know that I have the ability to make the world a better place. Teach me the patience and humility to realize that even small steps make a big difference.

Never Too Small To Star

"Even when I was little I was little," says David Eckstein. "I knew I'd never be tall." Yes, at 5' 6" and 165 pounds, the shortstop for the 2002 World Series champion Anaheim Angels might be mistaken for a batboy at times, but he has the heart and confidence of a giant.

Eckstein helps his baseball team win, and his teammates know he's the X-factor in their lineup. Like his team, the scrappy leadoff hitter has defied expectations and is modest to a fault, claiming, "Everything I do is ugly." The youngest of five children, he returns home in the off-season to Florida to live with his family. Still single, he doesn't smoke, drink, swear or miss Sunday worship.

If there's any single philosophy David Eckstein has lived by, it's this: "If you believe in yourself, you can do it."

That's a positive thought to remember when life has got you down. No matter one's size, anyone can live tall.

Stand firm in your faith, be courageous. (1 Corinthians 16:13)

Let my heart be strong and fearless, Lord Jesus.

The National Symbol

In June, 1782 the bald eagle became the official image on The Great Seal of the United States. Unfortunately, that honor did not keep it from being hunted and trapped; its habitat destroyed.

"The relationship between human development and the absence of bald eagles has been documented in various places across the country," said David A. Buehler, in *Birds of North America: Life Histories for the 21st Century*. Although the U.S. Fish and Wildlife Service downgraded its endangered-species status in 1995, the bald eagle is listed as threatened.

Their comeback requires caution and care. As we move into more open spaces, eagles face danger to their habitats from pollution and destruction of natural resources.

Bald eagles will never reach the 250,000 there were before European immigration and settlement. Still, the opportunity to protect and preserve our national symbol and one of God's beautiful creatures, is ours.

God said, 'let Us make humankind in Our image...and let them have dominion over the fish...the birds...the cattle, and over all the wild animals'. (Genesis 1:26)

Teach us respect for earth's creatures, Almighty Creator.

Shelter from Stress

Stress has been around as long as we humans. We have found ways to cope with it, such as exercise, aromatherapy, a hot bath, deep breathing. But in particularly troubled times, those simple aids are often not enough.

Instead, concentrate on what you can control, not on what you can not (like the economy, terrorism or war). In other words, take a break from the news.

Learn from adversity. Many people develop a greater awareness of just what–and who–is important to them. Family can take on a far greater significance than work, success or money.

Connect with the sources of your strength. That means your religious faith or a cause greater than yourself, as well as your loved ones. They are your support, your joy and your comfort as much as you are theirs.

Trust God–and take things one day at a time.

Rejoice in hope, be patient in suffering, persevere in prayer. (Romans 12:12)

Holy Wisdom, guide me in these challenging times.

Seeing Angels

Monica had been there through many health crises with her mom–this one would be the last.

A massive stroke on a June Monday ended in Claire's death that Friday. During that last week of her mother's life, Monica left her mom's hospital bed only for a few hours sleep. On the morning Claire died, Monica was again with her mother, returning home now with the task of telling her three-year-old daughter, Hannah, that her "Granny" was gone.

"God loves us all very, very much, and He loved Granny a whole lot," Monica told Hannah. "So when Granny got really sick, He decided to take her up to heaven to live with Him and the angels."

At Claire's funeral Mass, Hannah kept whispering her wonder at when the angels would come to take Granny to God. At the end of Mass, Hannah grabbed her mother's hand and pulled her closer. "I see them Mommy," Hannah said. "I see the angels."

A child saw; a mother believed.

He will send out the angels, and gather His elect from the four winds, from the ends of the earth to the ends of heaven. (Mark 13:27)

I put my trust in You, Lord, for I believe in Your mercy and love.

A Tomato Grows in Harlem

Harlem is probably one of the last places one would consider a great place to grow food.

Yet, thanks to the persistence and dedication of an ex-blues singer, Garden Number 8 at Frederick Douglass Boulevard in Harlem harvests tomatoes, corn, cucumbers, eggplant, okra and more.

Willie Morgan, the primary gardener, tills the one-quarter block lot with three other neighborhood retirees. In addition to delicious produce, the team's efforts seem to reap neighborliness as well. Their toil supports the community not only directly—in feeding the needy—but serves as a community focal point where elderly residents often convene for companionship and conversation.

When you see a vacant lot, do you see hopelessness or possibilities? Beautiful things can grow in the most unlikely places. Amazing things can spring forth from a positive outlook.

There is hope for a tree, if it is cut down, that it will sprout again, and that its shoots will not cease...at the scent of water it will bud and put forth branches like a young plant. (Job 14:7, 8)

Dear Lord, I pray for the courage and faith to think positively in all situations.

Climb Every Mountain

Rock climber Lynn Hill understands the meaning of adventure. She was the first person to succeed in climbing the famous Nose of El Capitan in California's Yosemite Valley "free," using only her hands and feet to make the difficult ascent, relying on her ropes strictly for safety.

"Though I realized that I could easily fall in my exhausted state," she wrote, "I felt a sense of liberation and strength, knowing that this was an effort worth trying with all my heart."

James Meigs, who wrote about Hill's achievement, says he can't think of a better definition of adventure than an effort worth trying with all your heart. He also thinks the element of doubt makes an adventure. "That uncertainty principle can be apt not just for climbing Mt. McKinley," he observes, "but also for a person going back to college, playing a concerto, or raising children."

Celebrate your life as an adventure.

God...makes my feet like the feet of a deer, and makes me tread upon the heights. (Habakkuk 3:19)

Jesus, let me embrace a spirit of adventure today.

Surprising Change

Major change can begin in surprising ways. In 1856, while trying to synthesize quinine, a malaria cure in short supply, William Perkin, an 18-year-old British chemistry student, found red crystals in the bottom of a test tube

Perkin thought about discarding the unneeded crystal residues but he was captivated by their "strangely beautiful colour" which we now call mauve. He tested the new pigment on silk and found it brilliant and resistant to fading.

While Perkin failed to produce quinine, he'd created the first artificial dye and things would never be the same in fashion, medicine, chemistry or commerce.

Don't be discouraged by presumed failure. Stay open to surprise and the possibility of change.

Endure everything with patience. (Colossians 1:11)

Remind me Lord that I am capable of changing things for the better in small ways and perhaps in more dramatic ways.

A Lovely Surprise

Inge Rudolph and Dudley Donaldson never expected to love and marry each other. In the 1970s Dudley and his wife Mavis were friends with Inge and supported her work as a lay missionary with Trans World Radio.

Eventually they lost touch with each other as Inge's work took her all over the world and Dudley and Mavis raised their two children.

Mavis died in 1995 after a year's struggle with ovarian cancer. Dudley experienced grieving and also became severely depressed. After counseling and medication, he recovered and began looking up old friends.

Dudley located Inge on the Internet and they began an intense e-mail and telephone relationship. When they met in person after 17 years they had to make some adjustments. Prayer helped them to get over the few rough spots. And their romance blossomed. They were married after only seven months.

Life is full of surprises. Cling to God.

The Lord will guide you. (Isaiah 58:11)

Help us not to be afraid to take risks, Jesus.

Maintaining Strong Bones

Although the human skeleton is an example of beautiful and sturdy construction, it grows weaker with time, more so when combined with neglect such as lack of exercise.

When we're about 30 years old our skeleton is at its heaviest and strongest. A bony filigree of slender, mineral-rich strut gives bone most of its strength, according to Adam Summers, assistant professor of ecology and evolutionary biology.

"Our bones develop from soft cartilage. Evidence...can be seen in the soft spot in the center of a baby's skull," said Summers. "Most of our cartilage is gradually replaced by bone, which becomes more and more mineralized and thus heavier." As we age things change. We lose bone density, becoming at risk for fractures.

Even though scientific studies hold the promise that we'll someday find ways to stimulate old bones to thicken, "take the stairs," advises Summers, "and keep lifting those weights."

Take care of your body, as well as your mind and soul.

Your hands fashioned and made me...like clay...You clothed me with skin and flesh, and knit me together with bones and sinews. (Job 10:8,9,11)

Help us to fully appreciate Your creation, God.

More Than a Smoky Highway

When some hear the words "New Jersey," they envision smokestacks and factories, and a turnpike tied up with traffic.

These stereotypes obscure the fact that New Jersey is home to scenic towns and memorable architecture. In fact, forty-nine of New Jersey's train stations are considered worthy of preservation efforts, and are listed on the National Register of Historic Places. They include the majestic Hoboken terminal, built as a railroad and ferry terminal in the Beaux Arts style with a Tiffany skylight.

And then there's the Gothic and Romanesque style of stations located in Red Bank, Netherwood and Madison, which stand out as historic buildings with distinct beauty.

Stereotypes judge by appearances and exclude facts. Re-examine your stereotypes. What can you discover about the people, states, nations around you?

Do not judge and you will not be judged. (Luke 6:37)

Sharpen my ability to detect harmful stereotypes, Jesus.

Prayer in a Petri Dish

Most medical investigation is pretty straightforward–give this group a pill, give that group no pill, and see who gets better. These days, prayer is receiving the same approach. One group gets prayed for, while the other doesn't.

While researchers acknowledge the benefits of participatory prayer–reciting the rosary, chanting a mantra–in lowering stress and blood pressure, they are split on the question of intercessory prayer or praying for others. For example, what should be the "dosage" of the prayer? Once a week? Every day? What should be prayed for, especially in the case of grave illness where there is little hope for recovery? And many physicians don't feel religion should have a spot on a patient's chart.

Medical debates aside–and while scientific studies continue to address the question of prayer's power–most patients and their families "believe." To that, let's say, "Amen!"

Stay awake and pray. (Matthew 26:41)

Father, send us Your healing love, and grant us Your peace.

Bringing its Glory Back

It's almost 200 years old and is currently undergoing an $18 million facelift. What is it?

It is "Old Glory," the original three-story high flag that flew over Fort McHenry during the War of 1812 and that inspired Francis Scott Key to write our national anthem, "The Star-Spangled Banner."

The conservation effort includes the painstaking process of removing and replacing more than a 1.7 million stitches. Thanks to the Save America's Treasures effort, the flag will allow future generations to appreciate "Old Glory" for years to come.

Support programs that preserve our national heritage, either by volunteering, writing letters or speaking out. There's much to be learned; much to be preserved. Most importantly, there is much of which to be proud–as well as much that needs to be improved.

Let justice roll down like waters, and righteousness like an ever flowing stream. (Amos 5:24)

May we have greater respect for our country, Lord.

Moses' Biggest Battle

He's always played larger than life characters, such as Moses and Judah Ben Hur, so when Charlton Heston announced that he was suffering early symptoms of Alzheimer's disease, it shocked people. A man of great energy, the controversial actor said, "I am neither giving up nor giving in. But it's a fight I must someday call a draw."

Married for 58 years, he and his wife, Lydia, are maintaining a positive attitude. Hearing from former First Lady Nancy Reagan, who has cared for her Alzheimer's stricken husband, Ronald Reagan, since 1994, helped them.

Alzheimer's disease plays no favorites. It affects about four million Americans–and their loved ones.

Whatever burdens come your way, ask God for the strength and grace to live your days as well and as bravely as you are able.

The Lord created medicines out of the earth, and the sensible will not despise them. (Sirach 38:4)

With You at my side, I can hold my head high, Lord.

Joy to the World

"Feeling joyful is a basic human need," says Leigh Anne Jasheway. Here are some of her ideas for ways to put more joy in your life.

One: search for jubilance. "Don't wait for it to come knocking at your door," she advises. "Seek out things that give your life meaning and purpose."

Two: write down all the things that bring you pleasure. By comparing it to the reality of your daily existence, you may see obvious steps you can take to increase your joy.

Three: heed the call of pleasure. "The world's happiest people are those who have found what they are meant to do in life and are doing it every day," she asserts.

Four: bring joy to the world. "The more you work to bring joy to everyone, the more your life will feel truly blessed and enriched," Jasheway concludes.

A modern writer said that we are lutes strung for joy. Is your life a song of joy?

The fruit of the Spirit is love, joy, peace, patience, kindness, generosity, faithfulness, gentleness, and self-control. (Galatians 5:23)

Remind me, Spirit, how to be my best self.

Divine Play on the Ball Field

"Do you think they'll let me play?" Shaya asked his father.

The boy who had a learning disability wanted to be part of a ballgame that he and his dad were passing on a walk home.

That day, the boys did let Shaya play. At the first pitch, Shaya swung clumsily and missed. On the next pitch—a ball tossed softly toward him—Shaya hit a slow ground ball to the pitcher. The pitcher picked up the ball—and deliberately threw it far beyond the reach of the first baseman. Everyone cheered Shaya on to run—and he did, all the way to home plate.

"I believe that when God brings a child like Shaya into the world, an opportunity to realize the Divine Plan presents itself in the way people treat that child," the youngster's father said of the experience. "That day the boys from both teams helped bring a piece of the Divine Plan into this world."

Every parent faces many challenges. We can help by giving support to them—and their children.

You shall not revile the deaf or put a stumbling block before the blind. (Leviticus 19:14)

Give me a share of Your wisdom, Master, that I may know the right path to choose.

Grand Uncle Daddy

Kelli was three when she fell down a flight of cement steps. No one was watching her—her mother Kerri and grandmother Becky had serious drug problems.

A social worker at the hospital the night Kelli was brought in telephoned Jim Howard, Becky's brother, telling him that unless he agreed to take responsibility for his grand niece, she would be placed in permanent foster care.

"I knew immediately that I would take her," Jim said.

For Kelli, moving in with her grand uncle Jim meant getting her childhood back. For Jim, it meant seeing the world in a whole new way—this bachelor even learned to iron.

Today, seven years later, both Kerri and Becky are drug free and share a home with Kelli and Jim. And although Kelli calls him Uncle Jimmie, the handmade Father's Day card on his refrigerator suggests that, for purposes of the heart, Jim is Kelli's dad.

Do everything in the name of the Lord Jesus. (Colossians 3:17)

Father, You are always with me, filling my heart and soul with Your love.

Don't Pretend

Novelist Siri Hustvedt once reflected on a fabled New York survival technique: Whatever's going on, pretend it's not. It's a way of coping in a city where unpredictable things happen.

Yet Hustvedt offered an example of someone breaking the code. One day, while the novelist's daughter was riding the subway, a man began staring at her. His gaze was so persistent that Hustvedt's daughter became uncomfortable, and breathed a sigh of relief when the man left the train.

As the train left the station, though, the man screamed out, "I love you!" Hustvedt's daughter was mortified until a fellow passenger deadpanned, "It looks like you have an admirer."

His wisecrack, Hustvedt wrote, gave her daughter "a feeling of ordinary human solidarity."

Sometimes all a person in a moment of need requires is a simple human connection. Reach out to those around you. It'll often cost nothing more than a moment of your time.

**Those who are generous are blessed.
(Proverbs 22:9)**

Lord, help us to forge a connection with those around us.

Making Miracles Happen

Pauline Alexander, 76, doesn't work magic, but she does what she can and makes small miracles happen.

For 17 years, Ms. Alexander has worked with others to gather donated food, medicine, clothing and other goods and bring them to impoverished villages in India.

Although born in the Himalayas to a family in India's highest caste, Ms. Alexander's early life was difficult. Fortunately she was educated in the United States as a nurse.

Her work today is with people in what is considered the lowest caste. Their health problems are caused or exacerbated by poverty, hunger and drought. Alexander, who has taught nursing, set up health clinics and worked in refugee camps, almost retired once. But she heard a voice telling her "Your work is not finished."

Each one of us has work to do each and every day of our lives. Let's do all we can for as long as we can.

Tabitha...was devoted to good works and acts of charity. (Acts 9:36)

Let us value the works of all, Lord.

Hope Through Horses

Fourteen-year-old Meir Soffer goes horseback riding each week at Kensington Stables in Brooklyn, New York. Blind and autistic, he is one of many young people with special needs who gain self-esteem, responsibility and hope through horses.

Equine Assisted Growth and Learning Association therapist Lynn Thomas says that feeding, riding and caring for horses boosts confidence and helps develop the nonverbal communication skills and sense of responsibility of those with disabilities.

After his ride Soffer often gently kisses his horse's mane. The change and focus he has when riding amazes his father. "To a kid like this, a good feeling means calmness and serenity, and a lot of these kids don't get that so easily."

For some at-risk youth and disabled children, a horseback ride can give them the tools needed to get a leg up on life.

For all of us, a bit of calmness and serenity really help us get through the day.

God formed every animal of the field...and brought them to the man to see what he would call them. (Genesis 2:19)

Lord we share Your world with Your creatures. May we come to see them as our helpers and healers who deserve our respect and care.

A Kind of Success

Charles Goodyear invented what we now call vulcanized rubber, which revolutioned transportation and other industries. Yet he and his family never profited from his success.

Goodyear's story is one of tortured commitment. According to Charles Slack, who published a biography of Goodyear, *Noble Obsession*, the inventor left no stone unturned in his lifelong pursuit of transforming rubber into a useful resource. He sold his own children's textbooks to finance experiments he conducted in the family's kitchen, and was not unfamiliar with debtor's prison.

In 1839 he finally found scientific success. But, lacking business acumen, Goodyear watched as others claimed the glory and the profits that should have been his.

Long after Charles Goodyear's death, a young businessman named Frank Seiberling decided to honor the inventor's singlemindedness, which had so advanced the industry, by naming his own rubber company after Goodyear.

There are no guarantees in life, yet we need to stay true to ourselves and our purpose.

**Pay...honor to whom honor is due.
(Romans 13:7)**

Holy Spirit, keep us true to our purpose.

Finding Faith

Hundreds of young soldiers, including James, were sent to the treacherous mountains of Afghanistan after the September 11th attacks. At 19, he confronted horrible fears. Each day his family prayed, trying to find the faith that James would return to his home unharmed. Weeks passed without knowing if he had food to eat, if he was scared. His mother wrote letters to military officials requesting the whereabouts of her son. With no reply, the situation became even more devastating.

One afternoon, his sister received a phone call from a woman named Faith. She was the mother of Wally, also a marine, who had befriended James. Her compassion gave James' family the courage to endure the lonely months, and lit the way to a friendship between both families. Both James and Wally came home safely.

Whether military families or others in need of some comfort, people are yearning for kindness. Offer it freely.

Now faith, hope and love abide, these three; and the greatest of these is love.
(1 Corinthians 13:13)

O Lord, help us give the everlasting gift of friendship to those in need of love and companionship.

Logging on to Comfort

Nearly five million people take part in online support groups, many for medical reasons. Having conditions from diabetes to depression, they share encouragement and sympathy.

Participants can either use real-time chat rooms for conversations, or message boards where they post stories and questions. To find a reputable group, stick with sites with at least 50 members and an administrator—and always consult your physician before taking medical advice.

Online support can make a difference. "The interaction reduces isolation and helps people deal with their feelings," says researcher Morton Lieberman.

Mary Manion, 46, a band director from Medford, New Jersey, wrote messages late at night, after chemo for breast cancer. "There was always someone going through the same thing," she says. "We'd make jokes to get through the night."

The next time you need support, get in touch with someone who understands. Your burden will be lighter.

The God of all grace...will Himself restore, support, strengthen and establish you.
(1 Peter 5:10)

When I call to You, loving Lord, send me hope.

Don't Fence Me In

Peter Westbrook grew up in public housing in New York City. As a teenager, his mother steered him towards fencing as a way to channel his frustration and anger.

It was the right move. Westbrook earned a fencing scholarship to New York University, and won a bronze medal at the 1984 Olympic Games. His achievements spurred him on to help other youngsters.

Today he oversees 80 students at Manhattan's Fencers Club. Westbrook's foundation pays for trainers, equipment, and travel to competitions. While students in his club, most of whom live in poverty, pay just $20 a year, the arrangement helps them understand the importance of investing in themselves.

Before each practice, the kids gather to discuss their school work and turn in the essays Westbrook requires of them. His efforts have developed three more Olympians–plus a number of young people who go on to other accomplishments.

Someone needs your help. Someone needs hope.

Encourage one another. (1 Thessalonians 5:11)

Jesus, to whom can I give encouragement to today?

When Actions Speak Louder Than Words

Maid of honor Caroline Cole wanted her best friend Tawny Randall's bridal shower to be a tribute to the bride's commitment to community service. A traditional shower wouldn't do.

"In junior high, Tawny Randall fasted 36 hours for UNICEF; in high school, raked leaves for the elderly and volunteered in soup kitchens. She majored in social work and became a school guidance counselor," said Cole.

So Cole arranged for friends and family to build a house for Habitat for Humanity. It would be occupied by a single mother and her two children.

Randall got gifts such as a tool belt, gardening gloves and a trowel. But, "the best gift was the way my friends gave of themselves," said Tawny Randall. Their actions were gifts of loving service for the new homeowner.

What gift of loving service can you give?

The only thing that counts is faith working through love. (Galatians 5:6)

God, with Your grace may all of my actions speak of love.

Raising a Prodigy

Mary and Phil Mickelson, Sr. weren't trying to develop a golf prodigy. Their challenge, as parents, was to encourage their son's devotion to the game for which he had an obvious prowess while using golf to motivate and guide him.

Phil's parents reinforced two key points. First, no matter how good he became, he should always be modest and considerate. Second, he was to go to college. Even after winning a PGA event as an amateur, Mickelson chose to complete his degree rather than leave early for the pro tour.

Today, the Mickelsons see their son, his wife and their two grandchildren frequently, and follow his career on TV and in person. They enjoy watching their grandchildren learn the life lessons they once taught their son.

What a great gift for parents to see a child achieve, not only in the eyes of the world, but in developing good character!

**Give thanks in all circumstances.
(1 Thessalonians 5:18)**

I pray I've learned your lessons well, Father.

Some Friendly Advice

In the market for a new friend or two? Cindy Crosby, the mother of two children, offers several ideas for parents who want to help their children make friends. Many of them apply to adults as well.

Rather than wallowing in loneliness, take the initiative, invest the time and effort to have your child invite a friend to eat at your home or attend a special family outing. Making plans for an enjoyable lunch or afternoon together is a good step in the right direction.

"It's normal for kids to have friendships that don't work out," says Crosby. Most people are so busy they rarely get together with friends, let alone new acquaintances. "Making good friends can be a trial and error process."

It takes time and shared experiences for friendship to develop. Relax and enjoy yourself along the way.

Those who fear the Lord direct their friendship aright. (Sirach 6:17)

Let us find renewal in our friends, old and new, Lord God.

Club Help

A trend today among women is "giving" many a reason to say thanks. In the past few years, nearly 2,000 women have joined or organized giving circles, donating some $2 million to non-profit organizations each year.

"Spiritually, it's really powerful," says Pamela Rosin, who joined the Kitchen Table, eight young women of varying economic backgrounds committed to pooling their resources to help worthy causes. "We've taken a journey together by talking about our personal ideologies and looking at ourselves and how we want to make an impact in the world."

Says Stacy Palmer, editor of *The Chronicle of Philanthropy*, "This is a way for women to get together and to work together. Many of us don't have lots of opportunities to do that."

Good things can happen when we unite for others and for ourselves.

Be generous. (Judges 21:22)

Together we offer You our praise and our thanks for all Your gifts to us.

Going Beyond Punishment

Fedor Dostoevsky, the nineteenth century Russian novelist, is perhaps best known for *Crime and Punishment*, the gripping tale of a murderer who finds salvation atoning for his crime in prison. Dostoevsky used his own extraordinary experience as material for the novel's theme of redemption.

As a young author in St. Petersburg, Dostoevsky found company among a group of liberal radicals. Though he himself was politically indifferent, in 1849 he was arrested with other members of the group and condemned to death for conspiring to set up a printing press. On the day of his execution, Dostoevsky was spared from the firing squad by a last minute commutation by the Czar. He spent ten years at hard labor in Siberia.

Instead of growing bitter over this injustice, Dostoevsky developed a strong religious faith, and turned the punishment into an opportunity to become a better human being.

Turn your times of trial into times of growth and grace.

In the day of prosperity be joyful, and in the day of adversity consider, God has made the one as well as the other. (Ecclesiastes 7:14)

Holy Spirit, may I learn from adversity as much as from prosperity.

Woman's Best Friend: Freedom

Incapacitated by a stroke at age 24, Donelda Glenn had her freedom severely limited for 16 years. That is, until Freedom came into her life.

The fittingly named Freedom, a Black Lab, is a special skills dog trained at the Lions Foundation of Canada Dog Guides in Ontario.

With Freedom's assistance, Ms. Glenn can maneuver through doors and elevators. Freedom can retrieve items from the floor or remove a change purse from Ms. Glenn's handbag, place her paws on the store counter with the purse in her mouth, give it to the clerk for payment and return it to the handbag.

"Now there is an extra reason to get up in the morning," said Ms. Glenn. Although unable to walk, move her arms or speak forcefully, she has plans to move out of the nursing home where she lives. "I hope to have my own apartment."

It's amazing, what Freedom does...what freedom can do.

For freedom Christ has set us free. Stand firm, therefore, and do not submit again to a yoke of slavery. (Galatians 5:1)

God, teach us to value the gifts we've been given.

Summer Days

Today's children are used to being entertained. The days when mom said "Go out and play" seem a thing of the past. Safety is a legitimate issue, of course, and suburban sprawl does limit kids' ability to find things to do with neighboring playmates. Even "play dates" with friends are very structured and planned.

Parents, too, feel a greater burden to amuse their children and expose them to new and stimulating things. Yet, there are still timeless summer activities that are simply play: long games of Monopoly; eating ice pops on a hot summer evening; going barefoot; enjoying the swings at a playground.

Raising kids in any season is a true challenge. But it's worth the effort to help your kids one day recall their childhood summers with fondness and gratitude.

Old men and old women shall again sit in the streets...And the streets of the city shall be full of boys and girls playing. (Zechariah 8:4,5)

I know there is a time for everything, Lord, especially play.

One Important Note

In July 1958, Jack St. Clair Kilby wrote a relatively innocuous sentence in his lab notebook: "The following circuit elements could be made on a single slice: resistors, capacitor, distributed capacitor, transistor." That sentence would eventually bring him the Nobel Prize in physics.

Kilby grew up wanting to study at MIT, but he fell three points short on the entrance exam. After serving in World War II, he earned his degree in electrical engineering at the University of Illinois. Eventually he went to work for Texas Instruments, where he was assigned to wrestle with the day's most baffling concern in electronics, commonly known as "the wiring problem."

Unhindered by the knowledge of what wouldn't work, Kilby's ideas formed the basis of today's microchip. He played an important role in the development of the first handheld calculators, and helped birth a technological revolution.

Whatever kind of problem you are trying to solve, stay open and exercise your creativity.

Have confidence. (Job 11:18)

Give me confidence to pursue my dreams, Lord, even when failure slows me down.

A Positive Language

It was 1777, a year after the Declaration of Independence had been signed. The American colonies were engaged in the Revolutionary War with England.

During this difficult period, many members of the Continental Congress were somber and worried about the outcome. One complained to Sam Adams of Massachusetts that "the chance is desperate."

Adams replied, "Indeed it is desperate, if this be our language. If we wear long faces, others will do so, too; if we despair, let us not expect that others will hope; or that they will persevere in a contest from which their leaders shrink. But let not such feelings, let not such language be ours."

When times are toughest, determination and persistence are most essential to reaching our goals. "Think–and speak–positive." And entrust yourself and your plans to God.

Because of his persistence he will get up and give him whatever he needs. (Luke 11:8)

Blessed Trinity, keep me from getting discouraged when things get tough. Keep me going–towards You.

Summer Brothers

Nick and Robbie aren't family, but they feel as close as brothers. Unable to see each other during the year, the youngsters fall back into their comfortable friendship for two weeks each summer.

Robbie is from the Boston suburbs while Nick lives in Harlem. What brings Nick to Robbie's house is a Fresh Air Fund program called Friendly Town.

It is an escape for Nick to a different environment where he can climb trees, swim and even go fishing and camping. "Now he has something," Robbie's mother said, "a frame of reference that has broadened his horizons."

For the boys and their families, it is an opportunity for friendship that might not otherwise have been possible.

Friends can be found in many different places. You'll be surprised what you find when you look beyond your own backyard.

Three things...are beautiful in the sight of God and of mortals: agreement among brothers and sisters, friendship among neighbors, and a wife and a husband who live in harmony. (Sirach 25:1)

Lord, open our eyes to opportunities for friendship.

Everyday Grace and Goodness

Some days it seems we're blitzed with bad news. Take heart: acts of goodness still abound everywhere.

Maisie DeVore collected cans for thirty years. That helped build a public swimming pool in her hometown of Eskridge, Kansas. The town named the pool Maisie's Community Swimming Pool. Think about this: she accumulated 6 million cans over three decades. She sold homemade crab apple jelly in order to raise more money.

As news of what DeVore was doing got out, money streamed in from other sources. Actress Glenn Close, for example, who had starred in *Sarah, Plain and Tall,* which was filmed near Eskridge, donated $2,000. Eventually, DeVore had the money needed for the project, and the community pool opened in the summer of 2002.

DeVore is the personification of positive thinking. Her philosophy: "If you think you can't do something, you probably can't. But when I think I can, one way or another, I get it done."

Do what is right and good. (Deuteronomy 6:18)

My faith soars when people perform acts of kindness, Lord.

A Bigger Melting Pot

Cultural diversity is blossoming on New York City radio stations. Like the growing, changing metropolitan area it represents, radio there is learning how to blend rather than separate.

Radio is an expensive business and stations in the heart of a big city cost more than ten times what they would in the nearby suburbs. So, suburban stations with ethnic focuses are also growing as immigrants from Poland, India, Korea, the Caribbean and many other places prosper in New York.

What isn't happening, though, is division. These just-born stations know that they need to work together, sharing airtime bandwidth and operating expenses, if any of them are to succeed. Together, they can do what none of them could attempt alone.

Working together–that's a message from which we can all benefit.

Two are better than one, because they have a good reward for their toil. For if they fall, one will lift up the other; but woe to one who is alone and falls and does not have another to help. (Ecclesiastes 4:9-10)

Your love builds all things. Our intolerance can only tear down. Help us reflect Your love, Abba.

A Motivational Ultimatum

Kevin Parsons, a doctor of internal medicine, is waging a heroic battle against a rare and crippling neuromuscular disorder. It was his wife Hillary's ultimatum that inspired him to keep on living and fighting the disease.

In the mid-1980s, in a wheelchair at 38, his body ravaged by Lambert-Eaton Myasthenic Syndrome (LEMS), Parsons hit rock bottom. When he told his wife, the mother of their two children, that there was no reason to go on, she lost her patience. Telling him he still had a brilliant mind and could help himself, she warned him to shape up or she'd place him in a nursing home.

Today, thanks to an experimental drug treatment he is helping to pioneer, Parsons can walk on his own, drive a car and work several hours a day. As for Hillary Parson's tough-love challenge, "He just needed some motivation," she says.

Don't we all, at times? A loving but firm push can work wonders.

Love is patient...kind...rejoices in the truth. It bears all things, believes all things, hopes all things, endures all things.
(Corinthians 13:4,6-7)

Lord Jesus, Your love motivates me to carry on.

Make Yourself Happy

Making your life enjoyable is about spending less energy doing the things that don't bring you joy and more energy doing the things that do. *Family Circle* magazine even published a list of 60 ways to enjoy life. Here are a few:

- Instead of giving gifts, say or do something to boost someone's spirit.
- If it's uncomfortable, don't wear it.
- If you've had something on your to-do list for more than three months, remove it.
- Shop at small stores where you're not overwhelmed by the selection.
- Always start your day with the comics.
- Once a day ask yourself, "Am I having any fun yet?"
- If you haven't used it in over a year, toss it.
- Put a hammock in your backyard and use it.

Live small. Dream big.

The race is not to the swift, nor the battle to the strong, or bread to the wise, nor riches to the intelligent, nor favor to the skillful; but time and chance happen to them all. (Ecclesiastes 9:11)

Thank you, Lord, for the goodness in my life.

Teaching Tolerance

One young man who studied at Zeitouna, an Islamic university in Tunisia, said he went there with clear opinions about his faith.

However, his study of comparative religion, Darwin's theory of evolution and Freudian psychoanalysis challenged him to reconsider some ideas.

The young man concluded that, "Other religions are just as valid and have their own proofs." Another student approvingly said the university encouraged independent thinking.

The university is controversial. There are those who believe it is trying to invent a new religion and is not really teaching Islam. But university president Mohammed Toumi said, "The Quran has 125 verses that insist on religious freedom and that ask Muslims to respect others."

If you want your faith respected, respect others'.

The woman was a Gentile, of Syrophoenician origin. She begged (Jesus) to cast the demon out of her daughter. (Mark 7:26)

Jesus, who cured the Syrophonecian woman's daughter, the Roman centurion's servant and the Samaritan woman, cure our intolerance of others' faiths.

Passing Opportunities

A group of kayakers off the coast of British Columbia spotted a pod of Orca whales just 300 yards away. When their guide ordered them to back paddle, they wondered why he insisted they paddle away from what they'd come miles to see.

Throughout the trip, their guide had expertly led them along the area's coastline. They'd seen puffins, black bear and a plethora of sea life, including sea lions and dolphins. The group marveled at the guide's uncanny ability to predict strong currents; his skillful ability to read the tides. Still, his command to paddle away from the whales left them disappointed, sure they'd missed their chance.

A minute later, the Orcas reappeared, their huge fins within 20 feet of the group's tiny kayaks. The kayakers were treated to a spectacular display. Their guide had not failed them.

Sometimes stepping away from a problem or situation gives us a fresh perspective.

The glory of the stars is the beauty of heaven, a glittering array in the heights of the Lord. (Sirach 43:9)

Lord Jesus, help me have clarity in tough times.

All the Publisher's Men

Journalist Bob Woodward recalls a story about Katharine Graham, the publisher of *The Washington Post* at the time that Woodward and fellow journalist Carl Bernstein broke the Watergate scandal in that paper's pages.

In January 1973, seven months into the investigations of corruption in the Nixon administration, Graham invited Woodward and his managing editor to lunch with her. As Woodward updated her on the status of the investigation, Graham asked if he and Bernstein thought the full truth would ever be known. Well aware of the difficulties involved in getting proof, Woodward said that he wasn't sure. Graham's response was simple.

"Never?" Graham asked. "Don't tell me never." The answer galvanized Woodward. In the end, the Watergate investigations made Woodward and Bernstein famous as journalists and changed American history.

Don't give in to "never." You'll be amazed where determination can lead you.

By your endurance you will gain your life. (Luke 21:19)

Lord, grant us the strength and determination to make the world a better place.

The Duty of Freedom

In 2000, 89-year-old Doris Haddock, retired shoe factory worker, longtime activist and great-grandmother, set off on a walk. It took her 14 months to travel from Los Angeles to Washington, D.C.

Promoting the idea of national campaign finance reform, the New Hampshire native known as "Granny D" would not let desert heat or brutal blizzards stop her anymore than the arthritis or emphysema from which she suffered.

A believer in the power of the individual, she encouraged people to make a difference: "Your life in not trivial…It is real. You are a free man or woman in a land of free people who have served each other with dignity and sacrifice for many centuries. Do your duty to those who came before you. Do your duty to your own freedom and to the freedom of Americans to come."

Freedom has a price. Be sure to pay your fair share.

Take away from Me the noise of your songs… the melody of your harps. But let justice roll down like waters, and righteousness like an overflowing stream. (Amos 5:24)

Blessed Trinity, thank You for Your abundant gifts. Help me open my hands and my heart to Your children.

Filling in the Family Tree

Tim White is considered by some to be meticulous to a fault. A leading anthropologist, White once spent over five years piecing together a single skeleton. It sometimes takes him years to analyze and publish the results of his fieldwork studying the development of humankind and its ancestors.

Yet White's achievements are remarkable. Along with a collaborator, he is responsible for a radical restructuring of the human evolutionary tree. In the early 1990s, White co-discovered the 4.4 million-year-old *Ardipithecus ramidus,* which was then the oldest known human ancestor. Several years later, White's team unearthed the 2.5 million-year-old *Australopithecus garhi,* filling in a crucial gap in evolutionary history.

"He's the most exacting person I've ever met," anthropologist C. Owen Lovejoy says of White. "But that's what has made him so successful. He finds stuff that no one else can find."

Dedication and exactitude can lead to great achievement. Give everything you do your full attention.

You do well to be attentive. (2 Peter 1:19)

Lord, help us to pursue all of our ventures to their fullest extent.

Cool It!

Air conditioning is one of those things that people either hate or cannot live without. Even some of our presidents differed on the subject.

Franklin Roosevelt had a strong dislike of air conditioning of any kind, and never hesitated to say so. Needless to say, summers at the White House were never quite cool during his administration. On the other hand, Richard Nixon reportedly used the White House's air conditioning all year long, even to indulge in roaring fires regardless of the weather.

Whether you like it or detest it, air conditioning is one technological advance that changed the face of the American South, cooling sweltering homes in summer. The arrival of the air conditioner actually helped curb the exodus out of the South in the 1950s, and added to the region's revival.

Technology is so much a part of our lives, it's easy to take it for granted. Ever wonder how we'd get along without it?

I will protect those who know My Name. When they call to Me, I will answer them. (Ps. 91:14-15)

God, all things in life are gifts from You. Thank You for each and every aspect of my life that offers me comfort and safety.

Einstein's Penpals

Albert Einstein's theories and formulae are often approached with solemnity. But it once took a six-year-old to point out that the greatest scientific mind of the 20th century really should have considered a haircut.

Einstein received many letters from children during his lifetime. One child requested the formula for computing the speed of Satan's fall. Another asked that Einstein try not to lose his mind, as the writer and his friend had a bet on whether all geniuses eventually did.

Einstein often took such communications in stride. When one young girl expressed surprise that he hadn't lived 200 years ago, Einstein wrote, "...I have to apologize to you that I am still among the living. There *will* be a remedy for this, however..."

Sometimes it takes the attitude of a child to show us not to take ourselves too seriously. Even the most serious subjects have a lighter side—look for it in all you do.

Rejoice with song and singing. (Isaiah 35:2)

Lord, please help us to find the humor and pleasantness in all life gives us.

After Chicken Little Was Right

One evening, Sara Ban Breathnach learned that "Chicken Little," who predicted that the sky was falling, was telling the truth.

A ceiling panel in the restaurant in which she was eating fell, hitting her in the head. Bedridden, confused and disoriented for months, Breathnach found all of her senses had been affected, leaving her partially disabled for a year and a half.

During her sense-less period she wondered why God had singled her out for misery. But as her senses returned she began to "see" the lesson in it all.

"I was astonished and ashamed at my appalling lack of appreciation for what had been right under my nose," she says. She strives to savor life's textures, tastes, sights, sounds and aromas daily.

Recognize the amazing gifts God constantly gives you.

God did not make death, and He does not delight in the death of the living.
(Wisdom of Solomon 1:13)

Father, remind me that You delight in my wellbeing; grieve when I am physically, emotionally or spiritually wounded.

Nature's Way

Dr. Vandana Shiva is actively involved in promoting agricultural diversity in her native India.

Eleven years ago she helped found Nine Seeds. *Time* magazine reports that the group "encourages farmers to produce hardy native" crop varieties "that can be grown organically with natural fertilizer and no artificial chemicals."

True, more chemically dependent methods of farming have helped to break the cycle of famine and debt in developing nations. But Shiva believes genetic engineers should focus more on fostering seeds that will adapt well to local conditions.

A favorite saying of hers applies not only to the farmers and scientists with whom Shiva works, but also to anyone trying to bring light to their corner of the world. "You are not Atlas carrying the world on your shoulder," she observes. "It is good to remember that the planet is carrying you."

Respect the earth and its resources. Use them well.

Why is the land ruined and laid waste like a wilderness...Because they have forsaken My law...and have not obeyed My voice.
(Jeremiah 11:12,13)

Even as we work with fervor, Lord, remind us that this is Your Earth, not ours.

The Big Picture

Eugene Orowitz excelled as an athlete in high school, eventually winning a javelin scholarship to UCLA.

The young man dedicated himself to his sport, convinced it would be central to his life. And then, one day, it was all over. He tore a ligament in his shoulder, and never competed at the same level again.

Unsure of his future, Orowitz took a series of odd jobs including a stint as a door-to-door salesman. When a friend asked him for help preparing for an acting audition, Orowitz agreed, not knowing that his life was about to take a new turn.

Orowitz became known as Michael Landon, star of television series including *Bonanza, Little House on the Prairie* and *Highway to Heaven*.

He would later tell a reporter that tearing the ligament in his arm was the best thing that ever happened to him.

Pray to find the good in every event.

He will cover you with His pinions, and under His wings you will find refuge; His faithfulness is a shield. (Psalm 91:4)

Help me to trust in Your purposes, O God.

Talking Rocks?

Harriman State Park in southern New York State may not have the dramatic landscape of the Rockies or the Grand Canyon, but amid Harriman's topography, Dr. Alexander Gates has found his very own "Rosetta stone." And he wants to show it off.

Dr. Gates is working to establish a geological learning park within Harriman's 50,000 acres for students, teachers and "geotourists." Fellow scientists have said that Gates "made us realize that rocks can speak."

What a story these average-looking rocks can tell! Among rock layers that date back to after the last glacier retreated 12,000 years ago, Gates found a preliminary match that could link Harriman to Brazil.

Things that appear ordinary on the outside sometimes contain a wealth of information for us to discover. Take a closer look next time, you just might find your own Rosetta stone.

Do not judge by appearances. (John 7:24)

Lord, we are blessed with curiosity. Help us to use it well in our search for answers.

Lighten Up!

"God made us whole people," says Donna Lochner, a counselor and speaker. "Do we only bring our pious self to worship or do we bring our whole selves?" she asks.

Lochner points to Ecclesiastes 3:1, 4: "For everything there is a season, and a time for every matter under heaven…a time to weep, and a time to laugh."

Sr. Anne Smollin, author of *Jiggle Your Heart and Tickle Your Soul,* says humor plays an important role in relationships. "It unifies us. It brings a group together. Humor also has a healing component and can help get rid of anger."

Children seem to have an innate sense of this wisdom. According to Sr. Smollin, one study showed the average four-year-old laughs 400 times a day; adults, just fifteen.

Body, soul, mind—God created your whole being. Use it well and that means enjoying and celebrating your life.

A joyful heart is life itself. (Sirach 30:22)

Remind us of the importance of joy, especially when we're being too solemn, Lord.

A Home of Their Very Own

After 4,000 volunteer hours and $24,000 worth of fundraising, 62 volunteers from Denver's Calvary Church built Shirley Martinez and her two daughters a home of their own.

After fleeing an abusive father, Martinez earned a degree, got a job and provided for her daughters. However, a bedroom in her mother's basement apartment was not enough space for her family. That's when Habitat for Humanity stepped in.

Every Saturday, the 62 volunteers gathered with Ms. Martinez and hammered, nailed, and sawed away. After five months, the house had been completed. "I still can't believe it," Ms. Martinez said. "I thought I'd never be able to own my own home."

Through cooperation, determination and perseverance, volunteers were able to help fulfill the dream of Shirley Martinez. Working together always meets the highest aspirations.

Love the family of believers. (1 Peter 2:17)

Homelessness is a fact of life for many American families, Jesus. Show us how to remedy this tragedy.

Walking the Path of a Master

After six hours on the trail, a group of hikers, who were also artists, finally reached the distinctive rocks that signaled they were close to their destination. They were hungry and tired and daylight was fading. Time was running out to reach the Flume.

The Flume is a sheer rock canyon character-ized by rapids and waterfalls. It lies near the head of the Hudson River in northern New York State. A painting they loved by Alexander Helwig Wyant, who came to the area in the 1870's to recover from a stroke, was in their minds as they pursued their goal.

As the hikers reached their destination, they wondered if they would see what the artist saw there; feel what he felt.

Certainly they appreciated the sight enough to change their plans and spent the next day there, painting the beauty they found in their own way.

Throughout your day, keep your eyes open to beauty.

Do nothing without deliberation. (Sirach 32:19)

Light of Light, may Your will be made known to me.

Dad's the Boss

As the father of two daughters, ages 20 and 18, writer W. Bruce Cameron spends much of his time laying down the law–only to have his girls disqualify it immediately. As he says, "They just hit the 'automatic scorn' reflex."

Fact is, Cameron uses his life as a dad as fodder for his popular syndicated column, as well as for a recently published book, *8 Simple Rules for Dating My Teenage Daughter: And Other Tips from a Beleaguered Father.* His sardonic commentary on topics such as dating ("Not until I'm dead," he writes) has made him a favorite of parents nationwide. As his editor, John Temple, puts it, "For a parent, reading him lightens the load."

Being a parent isn't easy, and humor does help ease the burden of responsibility. The way Cameron sees it, "I'm the giant shock absorber between my daughters and life. And my job hasn't changed just because they no longer want my protection."

Fathers, do not provoke your children to anger. (Ephesians 6:4)

Father, help me to laugh each day as I raise my family.

Women Courageous

Lauren Cook has been participating in Civil War re-enactments for years. She began just the way the women who actually fought did–disguised as a man.

But Cook's knowledge of and passion for American history meant little to her fellow re-enactors once her gender was known. She was removed from the Antietam National Battlefield in Maryland because "women are not allowed to portray Civil War soldiers" at re-enactments.

Cook fought back, filed suit and won. Yet, a contentious debate about women's roles in the Civil War, and the contribution they made continued. She joined with military archivist DeAnne Blanton to write *They Fought Like Demons*, about the 250 known female soldiers on both sides of the U. S. Civil War. Incidentally, of the eight known women at Antietam, five were killed.

Discrimination is one of the many things that is evil in our world. Have the courage to work for justice.

Joshua...sent two...spies...(to) Jericho...Rahab...had...hidden them...as soon as the(ir) pursuers had gone out...she let them down by a rope through the window. (Joshua 2:1,6,7,15)

Help us work toward the Kingdom of Heaven by fighting for what's right, Spirit of Courage.

The Rewards of Volunteering

"We're the ones who get the blessing."

In making that statement, Tony Flowers of Vandalia, Illinois, was expressing the feelings of so many men, women and young people who derive much satisfaction from volunteering their time and talents to help others.

Flowers was one of the approximately 1,000 Southern Baptists who traveled to New York City to help in the clean-up after the 9/11 attacks had left buildings and lives in shambles.

Not only did they work without pay, they paid their own way. Volunteers were unconcerned that in many cases they were cleaning the apartments of fairly wealthy residents.

"These people have been traumatized," Paul Montgomery of Alabama told *The New York Times*. "It does not matter what level of affluence they had beforehand. They've suffered."

Time and again, volunteers show us that it really is more blessed to give.

A person is justified by works and not by faith alone. (James 2:24)

Inspire me, Holy Spirit, to spend a little time today doing something for someone else.

Working Towards More Fun

Barbara Schiller couldn't wait to go camping with her teenaged daughter, Serena. She imagined creating a deeper bond with her as they sat by the campfire under a moonlit sky.

Although the weather cooperated, Schiller says she and her daughter found themselves at each other's throats throughout the first day of their excursion. They argued about everything from where to pitch their tent to which trails to hike.

But that night they found something to laugh about and, hugging each other, were finally able to relax in each other's company.

How often do we find ourselves struggling to enjoy experiences we've looked forward to for weeks or months? When expectations are high, the behind-the-scenes demands of planning can interfere with our dreams.

Whatever is on your horizon, a family trip, a wedding, a weekend vacation or a holiday, make the commitment now to staying in the right–relaxed and hopeful–frame of mind.

My flesh will live in hope. (Acts 2:26)

Loving God, help us focus on our true priorities.

JULY 28

Attention To Detail

Ice Age paintings discovered in the 19th century in a grotto at Altamira in northern Spain proved so popular that eventually excessive tourist traffic threatened their very existence.

How could the public's desire to see the cave be satisfied while not irrevocably damaging the object of their admiration?

The cave was closed to the public in 1977. Studies were conducted to determine what environmental conditions would preserve the paintings.

Although public access would have to be restricted, a full-size replica was also created. With great attention to detail, artists would make a replica so realistic that it would allow visitors to experience as close to the real thing as possible.

Designed to instruct and entertain, the replica enables the public to see its heritage without putting the original at risk.

Develop your appreciation of art and history.

Let us now sing the praises of our ancestors. (Sirach 44:1)

God, instill in me an appreciation of the past; of the accomplishments of our ancestors.

Dreaming Big Dreams

Well before golfer Tiger Woods became world-famous, his father and he had many conversations about pursuing dreams and living responsibly. Said Woods, "My dad had a lot to do with my realizing I was a role model and that I needed to accept that responsibility."

A few years ago, Woods created the Tiger Woods Foundation to help others pursue their dreams. The foundation began its work on public golf courses, with Woods hosting clinics all over the country and raising money for public junior programs. The foundation has also reached kids in other ways, for example, funding programs like Target House, a residence for St. Jude Children's Research Hospital patients and their families.

Woods has dreamed big and accomplished much in his young life. As he knows, "Children everywhere need the encouragement to dream big dreams. I like to think we can help them do just that."

Start with dreams. End with action.

Encourage one another. (1 Thessalonians 4:18)

Lord, may I never stop dreaming.

Why Husbands Forget Anniversaries

Why do women so often remember emotional events—a first date or a marital spat—better than men? New research suggests it's partly biological; women's brains may be hardwired to both experience and recall emotional events more vividly.

Scientists at Stanford did brain scans on 12 men and 12 women as they viewed nearly 100 neutral or dramatic images. The subjects were later tested on which images they remembered. The two groups scored about the same on the neutral images, but women were likelier to recall the dramatic pictures.

Seeing the images and encoding the memories activated two parts of the brain in men and nine in women, suggesting the process is more complex in women. "I guess this gives men an excuse if they forget their anniversary," quipped researcher Turhan Canli. "Blame it on biology."

Spouses need to make a constant effort to remember—and respect—the things that are important to each other.

Enjoy life with the wife whom you love. (Ecclesiastes 9:9)

Holy Spirit, fill spouses with love, patience and tolerance.

Putting Persistence in Its Place

What attributes make somebody successful? Ability? Intelligence? Upbringing? Sheer good fortune?

According to President Calvin Coolidge, "Nothing in the world will take the place of persistence. Talent will not; nothing is more common than the unsuccessful person with talent.

"Genius will not; unrewarded genius is almost a proverb.

"Education will not; the world is full of educated derelicts.

"Persistence and determination alone are omnipotent. The slogan 'press on' has solved and always will solve the problems of the human race."

Certainly, people need a combination of factors to achieve their goals. But there is no doubt that little of value is ever accomplished without simple dogged determination. "Press on" is not a bad slogan for anyone who wants to succeed in doing good.

Be persistent. (2 Timothy 4:2)

Guide me, Blessed Trinity, in doing all that is right. Grant me the resolve to stick to my efforts so that I may accomplish good according to Your will.

Just a Minute, Please

Americans are obsessed with time. Writer Jennifer Ackerman ponders this preoccupation when she asks how many of us define success–even on weekends–by the amount of things we 'get done' within a certain time span? How often do we find ourselves turning down a pleasurable get-together with a friend for lack of 'free' time?

If you find that you must be ill in order to take time to read a book for pleasure; if you hurry your children through breakfast "in a frantic scramble to fill backpacks," you may be missing the stuff life is made of, says Ackerman.

It took a serious health scare to end Ackerman's own obsession with time. Now she views time in a "circular fashion" in which hours and minutes unfold, revealing the beauty and wonderment of the universe over and over again.

Each moment is precious–how and where we choose to spend our time is significant.

For everything there is a season, and a time for every matter under heaven. (Ecclesiastes 3:1)

Holy Spirit, enlighten me to my life's true calling.

Entertaining Violence?

In the wake of the September 11 terrorist attacks, our lives have changed in many ways. Our wildest imaginings about what human beings are capable of was proved not to be as far-fetched as we had thought.

Even our beliefs about what is right and wrong in pop entertainment seem open to question. At first, people weren't interested in any distractions, but over the days and weeks that followed, folks started to enjoy simple diversions again—to go to the movies, watch a silly sitcom and attend a sporting event. Yet the many violent movies, computer games and videos that are available give us pause.

There are any number of wonderful ways to entertain and amuse ourselves without causing misery for another person or creature, real or imagined. Parents, for example, can say "no" to their kids "playing" with "toy" guns; destroying property with "blaster" water pistols.

It's important to teach and live in peace.

A harvest of righteousness is sown in peace for those who make peace. (James 3:18)

Divine Lord, embolden me to say no to violence with courage and love.

Do You Hear What I Hear?

Donna Geffen took her daughter to see a puppet show. The emcee handed the young girl a microphone and asked her what her name was. "Amanda!" she declared, with a beautiful smile.

"I got goose bumps," says her mother.

Just three months earlier, neither Amanda nor her mom would have even considered attending the puppet show. Neither would the family's father, Bruce. All were profoundly deaf.

Then the three family members received cochlear implants allowing them to hear.

The fourth family member, 12-year-old Matthew, who has always been able to hear, awakened his mother during a thunderstorm. "It was the first time in his life and my life that I could comfort him," Ms. Geffen says, "because I understood why it scared him."

Hearing, seeing, smelling, tasting, touching– our five senses–are God's gifts. Thank God for them. Cultivate them for the good of your soul, intellect, emotions and body.

The earth will be filled with the knowledge of the glory of the Lord, as the waters cover the sea. (Habakkuk 2:14)

Give me courage, God, to embrace the opportunities you bring into my life.

Blinky the Gangbuster

Blinky Rodriguez' 16-year-old son was killed by a gang gunning for rivals in California's San Fernando Valley.

Instead of seeking revenge, he started reaching out to gang members. One Halloween night he organized a summit for 1,000 guys from 75 gangs. He told them, "You're holding your own families hostage." They were responsible, he told them, for the bullets that missed their targets and killed grandparents, little sisters and brothers.

Then he offered an alternative activity—football—and they responded. "It's harder to shoot guys that you'd just played a game with," he reasoned. In the following year gang murders dropped from 56 to two.

Rodriguez is now working with a new generation who have discovered the lure of the streets. He lost a son but continues to save the sons of many.

Do not give your heart to grief. (Sirach 38:20)

Prince of Peace, help me to conquer hatred with love; evil with good.

Stone by Stone

The National Cathedral is more than a historic landmark to fifth and sixth grade students who live in the Washington, D.C., vicinity.

Thanks to Margie Ward, who directs the cathedral's Medieval Workshop program, middle school students are treated to hands-on experiences in stone carving, blacksmithing, sculpting, making stained glass and creating brass rubbings. "Awesome," is a word she hears frequently from her eager students.

At the end of her day-long adventure in the basics of building cathedrals, 11-year-old Claire McGowan described the National Cathedral as having a safe, comfortable, warm feel. Pressed to consider why, her reply was simple. "Because it's been loved by so many people," she observed.

Building a cathedral requires skill, sweat, stamina, daring and endless patience. Approached in the spirit of love, perhaps the experience is not unlike that of building a holy life.

Hate evil and love good, and establish justice. (Amos 5:15)

Heavenly Father, do not let me shy away from the demands of being constantly "under construction."

Personal Standards Define Our Life

What separates our modern life from that of our pre-Industrial Revolution ancestors? For one thing, industrial standards.

Defined as "something set up and established by authority as a rule," there are standards in things like clothing sizes, electrical voltages and spelling. We accept these standards as part of our lives today.

New standards are being set all the time, especially in technology and electronics. Consider DVDs. People from countries around the world can understand the onscreen displays because 141 languages have been assigned a standard four-digit number which companies have agreed to use. That allows the multilingual capability of the system to exist.

The standards of what we consider acceptable are constantly evolving as well. Sometimes for the better, such as in technology, sometimes not, considering the increased violence in music and movies. While we live with society's standards, it is important to develop our own personal standards which reflect the presence of the Holy Spirit.

The law of the Lord is perfect...sure...right... clear...pure...true and righteous...sweeter also than honey. (Psalm 19:7,8,9,10)

I pray that I may have the courage to question and challenge what I feel is wrong, Lord.

Barbies, Tuna Sandwiches and Letters

Taylor Sevin has 200 Barbie dolls, enjoys tuna-salad sandwiches–and in one year, raised more than $8,000 for the Lombardi Cancer Center at Georgetown University.

Her motivation? Her dad Alan died of cancer there in 1999, at age 37; Taylor was just 7.

Father and daughter were inseparable since birth, recalls her mom, Kym. In fact, when her husband was dying, it was only after hearing Taylor's voice on the telephone that he finally surrendered to death.

Just before Christmas the year her dad died, Taylor approached her mother about her fund-raising. The Maryland youth wrote to everyone in the family address book, asking for help. Since then she's approached classmates, neighbors and friends.

"I didn't want other children to be as sad as I was," she says, explaining the reason behind her efforts on behalf of life, done in memory of her dad.

How can you reach beyond your own pain to help others?

The memory of the righteous is a blessing. (Proverbs 10:7)

I recall Your goodness, Creator, and offer You praise and thanksgiving.

Modern Day Shepherds

Shepherds still work in the deserts of California and Texas. Under a federal guest worker program, workers mostly from Peru and Chile, work 90 hours a week for less than minimum wage.

Miles from civilization, these workers live in conditions that can be described as difficult at best. Completely dependent upon their employers for food, mail and any contact with the rest of the world, they live, as shepherds always have, in isolation, with little human contact.

Ranchers deny that shepherds are mistreated. Still, activists are working to pass legislation to bring working conditions and wages up to reasonable standards.

Angels announced Jesus' birth to shepherds. Shepherds in turn told others of Jesus' birth.

Who has shepherded you? Do any of them need your help?

The Lord is my shepherd, I shall not want. He makes me lie down in green pastures, He leads me beside still waters. (Psalm 23:1-2)

Jesus, You are my Shepherd. Please teach me to shepherd others as You continually help me.

A Place of Solitude and Sanctuary

People do need people. They also need solitude, perhaps never more so than during artistic pursuits.

The noted artist Winslow Homer found refuge in a Maine cottage within earshot of pounding ocean waves. Some of his Yankee neighbors and the New England scenery would eventually be captured in his watercolors and oils.

Homer "exulted in high winds, lashing waves, and big snows," writes Robert M. Poole, a retired editor at *National Geographic.* "He thrived in the isolation of winter."

He was known to sit alone at a window for hours, "just watching things," said Doris Homer, a niece by marriage, who was still giving tours of the cottage in her nineties.

According to Poole, Homer was fortunate to have "discovered the work he was meant to do (and) the place he was meant to do it."

Have you?

There is...a time to keep silence, and a time to speak. (Ecclesiastes 3:1,7)

Encourage creativity, Divine Master.

Teen Sleuth? Blue Roadster? Nancy Drew

Generations of youngsters stayed up late, flashlight under the covers if necessary, to find out how Nancy Drew solved "The Secret of the Old Clock" or other absorbing mysteries.

Perhaps Mildred Benson also stayed up puzzling out the same mysteries. Not as reader though, but as writer. Mildred Wirt Benson, aka Carolyn Keene, wrote 23 of the first 30 Nancy Drew novels.

Benson said of Nancy Drew, "She's a legacy, a spiritual treasure passed on." And she added that Nancy Drew was appealing because she was tough, smart and adventurous.

The same might be said about the author who became a commercial pilot, as well as a trained journalist. Incidentally, she worked on a newspaper until her death at age 96.

Use the opportunities God gives you to benefit our world as well as yourself.

Give her a share in the fruit of her hands. (Proverbs 31:31)

Grant women and men courage, Redeemer, in the presence of life's dangers, adventures and mysteries.

New Discoveries

Scholars had searched for decades without results for the jade they knew to have been most valued by the early civilizations of the Americas, but whose source was lost.

It took a violent hurricane ripping through Central America in 1998 to expose the ancient veins of jade. Thousands of people were killed in the resulting floods and landslides. Much pain and suffering resulted.

But the jade discoveries in Guatemala astounded museum specialists, geologists and other scientists. Scholars hope to continue studying the sites. The more they look the more they learn, not only about the geology but about the lives of the early inhabitants of South America.

At times, we, too, search for a long time to understand some truth about ourselves. Sometimes it takes a great personal upheaval before we can see that truth clearly.

Jesus said...'If you continue in My word, you are truly My disciples; and you will know the truth, and the truth will make you free'. (John 8:31-32)

Give us courage, Blessed Trinity, to pursue the truth wherever it leads.

Sorry Seems to be the Hardest Word

Righting a wrong is never easy. Mr. Song, a middle-aged Chinese businessman, couldn't offer a sincere apology to his own father. He turned to The Tianjin Apology and Gift Center, whose motto is "We say sorry for you," for help.

While phrases like "excuse me" or "I'm sorry about that" are common among Westerners, apologizing is an act uncommonly offered or accepted in Chinese culture. For example, officials never publicly apologized to the millions who were beaten or killed during the country's Cultural Revolution, even though they have called the time "a disaster."

After five attempts by apology company representatives, and after years of estrangement, Mr. Song the businessman and Mr. Song the elder have been happily reunited.

Nothing replaces a sincere heartfelt apology.

A rich person does wrong, and even adds insults; a poor person suffers wrong, and must add apologies. (Sirach 13:3)

God, help me remember to place You in the middle of my conflicts and difficulties that through You I may find resolution.

A Summer Camp That Saves Lives

Did you ever think of summer camp as a lifesaver?

Judith Jenya did. The lawyer, who was born to European refugees, (her father an escapee from Hitler's Germany, her mother from Stalin's Russia) was told by a Croatian orphanage administrator that he hated humanitarian types like her. He said they "come here, take photos and feel sad and no one does anything." Jenya was different.

She started summer camps for Bosnian and Croatian children in the midst of the war that raged there. For two weeks, the children leave the horrors of war behind. "The things these children have experienced we'll never truly know or understand," but she's given them a chance for some happy memories. Next on her agenda: a California summer camp for refugees.

Next time you think that no one is doing anything to solve a problem, ask yourself what you can do.

It would be better for you if a millstone were hung around your neck and you were thrown into the sea than for you to cause one of these little ones to stumble. (Luke 17:2)

Jesus, watch over those children who have lost their innocence due to their suffering.

On Goodness and Kindness

Computer science professor David Gelernter nearly lost his life through a violent attack by the "Unabomber." He did lose his right hand and eye. And he suffered other serious injuries in the 1993 explosion.

But he never gave up on himself–or other people. Indeed, he found the goodness of people after the bombing completely overwhelming. In his book, *Drawing Life: Surviving the Unabomber*, Gelernter says, "If you insert into this weird slot machine of modern life one evil act, a thousand acts of kindness tumble out."

Sometimes, it takes being confronted by evil to appreciate the power of goodness. Yet, it is the little choices we make every day that make us capable of generous compassion as a way of life. When you wake up every morning, you have new opportunities to love and to do good. Make the most of them.

Be hospitable, a lover of goodness. (Titus 1:8)

Holy Spirit, inspire me to do good, to be good, to be Yours.

A Juggling Lesson

Here's an old tale recounted by Harry Paige in *Catholic Digest* that bears retelling. A street juggler, a simple man of faith, would perform for audiences on the crowded streets of Paris for a scattering of coins, earning barely enough to keep him alive.

On one feast day to honor the Virgin Mary, one of the priests at Notre Dame Cathedral discovered this man juggling balls and rings before a statue of Our Lady. When the priest reprimanded him for his actions, the juggler replied: "I am sorry, but I have nothing else to offer Our Lady on this, her day, but the talent I live by, a talent that the Lord has graciously given me."

The lesson is clear: It is not what we do that makes us holy. We make holy what we do.

Everything may be an offering, especially our humble tasks, our prayers and our sufferings.

What does...your God require of you? ...To walk in all His ways, to love Him, to serve the Lord your God with all your heart and with all your soul, and to keep the commandments. (Deuteronomy 10:12-13)

Bless the work of my hands, Lord, that what I do may offer You praise and others joy.

This Way to the Shipwreck

Shipwrecks often attract unwanted scuba divers and souvenir hunters who strip valuable items from historically significant sites.

Because of this, according to *Archeology* magazine, some countries have made it illegal for recreational divers to visit historic wrecks.

But the Vermont Division for Historic Preservation took a different tack. It established an underwater preserve in Lake Champlain, which has "the best collection of historic shipwrecks in the country," according to Art Cohn, Maritime Museum director.

Professionals studied and documented the wrecks and removed important artifacts. Informational booklets have been made available and visits, with a few rules, allowed.

"Divers have been overwhelmingly cooperative," said Cohn. Many now seem as invested as archeologists in preserving the wrecks for all to see.

Education opens doors to past and future.

Teach me the way I should go. (Psalm 143:8)

Lord God, inspire us to study, respect and learn from the past.

Taking a Stand on a Billboard

Driving through Los Angeles, Judy Gruen was astonished to hear her seven-year-old practice his reading skills by reciting the suggestive ad on a billboard.

"That day I decided to take a stand," says Gruen.

The mother of four called the retailer responsible for the billboard. She was happily surprised to hear that others, too, had registered their protest; the entire campaign was soon scrapped.

In the five years since that first incident, Gruen has succeeded in getting numerous offensive billboards removed from her community. Her method: a polite but firm telephone call or letter, and patience–always listening to the other side.

When told she's "the only one" complaining, Gruen remains undaunted. "I tell them that even if that's true, it doesn't mean I'm wrong," she says, asserting her actions are "a powerful testimony to the difference every one of us can make in our own communities."

Stand up for your beliefs.

The Lord...confirms a mother's right over her children. (Sirach 3:2)

Your Word, Father, brings Light and Love to a waiting world.

You've Got to Have Friends

Everybody needs friends, but friendship isn't always easy. Our lives come with their own demands. We can't always devote the time and attention to friends that we'd like to, or that our friends might desire. So what do you do when a friend demands more than you are able to give?

For example, you spend hours listening to the friend who constantly calls for support, but after some weeks or months see that he or she isn't feeling better. When a friend is struggling with personal issues, work, marriage, children, or finances, sometimes the kindest and most loving thing we can do is to encourage him or her to get professional help.

A counselor or therapist might have just the skills your friend needs to work through problems.

Also, tactfully, lovingly, let your friend know that while you can't always be there for them, God is always with them. Remember your friend in your prayers.

Because you have made...the Most High your dwelling place, no evil shall befall you...He will command His angels...to guard you in all your ways. (Psalm 91:9-10,11)

Father, remind me that You and I are my brothers' and sisters' keepers; my friends' keepers.

Hidden Treasures

You never know when you'll strike gold – or at what age. To wit, fifth-grader Bingham Bryant, who, thanks to his interest in Greek mythology, decided to discover more about a Victorian painting at a local library that piqued his youthful curiosity.

The ten-year-old asked his father, an antiquities dealer, for help in finding out the value of the painting, *The Fate of Persephone,* which, in 1946, was valued at only $200. As a result of their investigation, which took two years and involved tracing the painting's history and worth, *Persephone* sold in London for a whopping $560,000.

Young Bingham, who received a finder's fee for his efforts, is now at a British boarding school, but says he'll be keeping an eye out for other hidden treasure.

Life is full of surprises, and one person's garbage might well be another's gold. It pays to look deeper into anything that interests us.

The eye desires grace and beauty. (Sirach 40:22)

Help me, Creator, to never lose my appreciation for beauty.

If Only...

Few adults can honestly say they've lived their lives with no regrets. After surveying thousands of people, researchers came up with a clear list of the most common regrets:

- Not getting a better education. In 50 years of research, this regret is always at the top of the list.

- Marrying the wrong person. For older women, especially, often married early and dependent on men economically, this is a particular problem.

- Spending too little time with family. Focusing on careers in lieu of spending time with children and spouse is a common regret.

However, experts say there is a positive side to regrets. They tell us that something is wrong. Focusing on the reasons behind them can teach you about yourself and help you make important decisions about your priorities now and in your future.

Judge with right judgment. (John 7:24)

Lord, strengthen me to make healthy choices, with my priorities in focus.

From Rail Station to Music Junction

A ghost town. That's how people referred to the East Texas hamlet of Sacul. "This was a busy place when I was growing up," recalls lifelong resident Novis White, "but the train quit coming through and everything dried up."

Tired of passing by the overgrown town square, White gathered several friends and eventually the whole town and began chopping away at the vines and weeds. Somebody suggested they build a pavilion. To raise the money, the town held annual folk festivals. After four years, there was enough to build a community center and to convert a drugstore into the "Sacul Opry."

Today, hundreds of musicians and spectators come to Sacul. "If you like bluegrass, this is the place to be," says guitarist Billy Jernigan.

The one-time ghost town has turned into a "happening place" and it all started with the work of one person.

To each is given the manifestation of the Spirit for the common good. (1 Corinthians 12:7)

Send Your grace to us, Lord, to transform the everyday into the divine.

No Jaws Here

Sharks have long been one of the most feared creatures in the sea. So when they showed up in waist-deep water off Maine's Wells Beach, people were concerned.

Beachgoers were called in from the water and prohibited from swimming for three days while the Mako and porbeagle sharks fed on a nearby school of mackerel. Despite the aggressive reputation of sharks and the intense media coverage of shark attacks, the mood on the beach remained surprisingly calm.

"The calmness means people are appreciating what's out there, they're respecting it," said Holly Martel Bourbon, senior aquarist at the New England Aquarium. She adds that people are becoming more educated about sharks.

With education and respect, fear has no chance. Just ask the vacationers on Wells Beach.

Do not fear or be dismayed. (Deuteronomy 31:8)

Giver of life, help us respect and honor all the living creatures with which we share our world.

Who Is a Hero?

Is a hero someone who persists and helps others despite the hardship?

It may be hard to agree on one definition of hero but many would put Max Cleland into the category. He lost one arm and both legs in 1968 while serving as a soldier in Vietnam, then went on to a life in public service, most recently as U.S. Senator.

After returning from war, Cleland felt helpless. "I felt I had made no progress in a year of arduous effort to readjust and reclaim my life. I was still in the hospital, still struggling, fighting the same demons. And I just cried those sobs of despair. I realized this was no game. It was either it or me. And I had to fight."

Cleland found inspiration in the lives of Jesus, George Washington, Franklin Roosevelt and Winston Churchill. He loves the quote "Never give in. Never. Never. Never."

It's a good saying to remember when times are rough.

The Lord will be a light to me. (Micah 7:8)

When I am in the darkness of despair, Jesus, show me the way out of helplessness and hopelessness.

The Puffin Patrol

Every August millions of pufflings (newborn puffins) leave the cliffs of Heimaey, an island off the south coast of Iceland. They fly over the north Atlantic at night using the moon to navigate. Unfortunately some become confused by the streetlights of Heimaey and instead of flying out to sea, fly into the town, landing on the streets.

But every night that month the local children form a Puffin Patrol, an annual search which has been in effect for generations. Accompanied by their parents, youngsters walk through town searching for stranded pufflings. As they find them, the children bring them indoors for the night.

The following day all the rescued pufflings are brought to the seashore, pointed in the right direction and "thrown" into the air. Some fly off at once, while others land in the water and take off from there.

What better way to thank God for His wonders than to care for them.

By the streams the birds of the air have their habitation; they sing among the branches. (Psalm 104:12)

Creator of the universe, teach us to respect all life.

Table for 240, Please

Every day, hundreds of adults and children come to Pasaje Pernambuco in Buenos Aires for a warm meal, served with a glass of soda and a reassuring smile.

Rubén Donadio and his wife, Hilda, opened the community center and soup kitchen 12 years ago in this suburb of Argentina's capital. Hilda Donadio started in her own kitchen, giving a glass of milk to each poor child in the neighborhood.

The need grew and a bigger place was opened. After Sra. Donadio died of a brain tumor in 1999, Rubén continued her mission. With a team of volunteers, he feeds lunch to 240 people each day. On Saturdays, children come for tutoring.

"I feel great with what I do," says Rubén. "I love to cook, and I love to help."

Every day, there are more than 200 people who love the fact that Rubén and Hilda Donadio wanted to–and did–help.

You can always choose to do good.

Come, you that are blessed by My Father...for I was hungry and you gave Me food, I was thirsty and you gave Me something to drink. (Matthew 25:35)

You fill my life with so many gifts, Master. May I use them wisely, offering You praise.

Tiny Swimmer, Big Splash

Even the smallest person can make a big impact.

In 1919, many thought women should not dive because it would injure their health. Not allowed to use indoor pools with diving boards, Aileen Riggin Soule instead practiced in a tidal pool where conditions mimicked those of an Olympic diving pool.

Despite these obstacles, Soule, a 4-foot-7 inch 14-year old, became the youngest American Olympic Gold medalist. Soule won the gold in women's springboard diving at the 1920 Olympics in Belgium. She was in the 1924 Olympics and turned professional the following year.

Aileen Riggin Soule continued swimming and even set six world records for her age group when she was 85 years old.

Life offers so much. Don't be afraid to dive right in!

To each is given the manifestation of the Spirit for the common good. (1 Corinthians 12:7)

God, when I am discouraged, strengthen my resolve and soothe my fears.

Music Lessons

Born in Paris, France, world famous cellist Yo-Yo Ma moved with his parents to New York City when he was seven years old. A few years later he began taking lessons from cellist Leonard Rose.

As he listened to Rose play, Ma recalls thinking: "How can you make such a gorgeous sound? How can anyone do that?" "I wanted to play just like him," he says. "But I came to realize that's not what music is about."

Rose told his young student, "I've taught you many things, but now you have to go off and learn on your own." According to Ma, that was perhaps the greatest lesson his gifted, patient teacher taught him. "The worst thing you can do is say to yourself I want to be just like somebody else," explains Ma. "You have to absorb knowledge from someone else, but ultimately you have to find your own voice."

Be brave enough to sing with your own voice.

A disciple is not above the teacher. (Luke 6:40)

I sing out with joy, Master, for You have blessed me with the gift of a new day.

Beating Terrorism by the Book

Rev. Khalid Rashid Asi, a Pakistani Roman Catholic priest, believes he's found one thing more powerful than terrorism–education.

"Our motto is 'each one, teach one'," says Rev. Khalid. "Every person is called to make a difference through his or her witness to the faith to at least one other person."

In the village school some 1,000 Pakistani children, Muslim and Christian, are educated side-by-side. "Hopefully, they will grow in love and acceptance of one another," he says.

For this priest education is the hope both for the children's future and for future peace of Pakistan, a nation that has had its share of terrorism and violence.

Rev. Khalid says, "Education is, for us, the way to peace and, hopefully, the end of terrorism."

Let's learn respect and acceptance of those whose religion, race, ethnic origin or country of origin are different from ours.

All Scripture is inspired by God and is useful for teaching. (2 Timothy 3:16)

Give me courage, Father. In difficult times, be my strength.

A Fly Fishing Nun

Fly fishing, a sport that gained wider appeal after the book and movie, *A River Runs Through It,* remains largely a male-dominated sport.

But did you know that the first fishing manual, written in the English language in 1421, was authored by a woman?

What's more, Dame Juliana Berners was the prioress of a Benedictine monastery. And her book, *A Treatise of Fishing with an Angle* illustrates Dame Juliana's extensive knowledge of the subject. Her book goes into minute detail on constructing a rod and creating flies with a variety of materials.

Dame Juliana believed that the sport promoted a merry frame of mind and she encouraged participation "for your enjoyment and to procure health of your body and, more especially, of your soul."

People are complex and wonderfully unique—and so are God's other creatures.

A woman who fears the Lord is to be praised. (Proverbs 31:30)

God, I thank You for Your amazing creations.

Field of Dreams

Gary Garner loved coaching his son Zack's Little League team until he caught sight of his daughter, Lindsay, watching from the stands.

"She was just sitting in her wheelchair with nothing to do," he remembers. "It broke my heart."

A few months later, Lindsay, who has muscular dystrophy, participated in a baseball game for kids with disabilities. The day was such a hit that Gary and his wife helped create what is now known as the Miracle League.

Aided by the fund-raising efforts of the Rotary Club, the Miracle League plays on a state-of-the-art, accessible youth baseball field next to three regulation fields in Conyers, Georgia. Challenged and able-bodied kids can interact comfortably.

A buddy program matches able-bodied kids with the special kids, and word is that the buddies and their new friends are enjoying lunch together at school, too.

Recognize that everyone is handicapped in some way and no one is perfect but all of us are human beings.

You shall not revile the deaf or put a stumbling block before the blind. (Leviticus 19:14)

Take my small efforts, Creator, and multiply their effect.

A Friend for the End

Phyllis Farley thinks no one should die alone.

So with a few co-workers, Farley, chairwoman on the board of the Maternity Center Association in New York, took a birthing center concept, the doula, and founded Doulas to Accompany the Dying.

The program trains volunteer men and women as doulas (Greek for "women who serve") to be a combination friend, coach and confidant for the solitary terminally ill.

As a doula, Farley smuggled one patient's dog into the hospital for visits and found a good home for the animal. Farley stayed to comfort her patient even after she had lapsed into a coma.

In spite of the emotional toll, Farley remains steadfast in her support for her mission. "I want to see a program...where no one has to die alone and derelict."

Many of us are blessed with loved ones. How can we share these blessings with those less fortunate?

**I was sick and you took care of Me.
(Matthew 25:36)**

Redeemer, infuse us with courage and compassion in the face of death.

The Power of Hope

"You have to have hope," says Louise Ashby. "It keeps you alive." She knows from experience.

A decade ago, just after the model and aspiring actress had arrived in Hollywood from London, her face was horribly disfigured in a car crash. Today, 12 surgeries later, she's using her "million-dollar face" (that's about how much it cost to repair the damage) to help those who can't afford to fix their own.

Ashby is the unpaid spokeswoman for the nonprofit Facing Forward Foundation (FFF), which provides free or low-cost surgery for disfigured kids. The founder of FFF, Dr. Henry Kawamoto, was Ashby's surgeon. Her goal: raise $6 million.

Louise Ashby turned a personal misfortune into a positive force in her life. "My dream was to be an actress, but the reality is better," she maintains. "What I've been through has made me able to touch other people's lives. I can't be anything but grateful."

Have hope–and gratitude.

Be thankful. (Colossians 3:15)

Regardless of events, I will reach out, Holy Spirit.

In Your Dreams

Bestselling author Neil Gaiman built his reputation by writing the acclaimed comic series *The Sandman*, but his aspirations were almost squelched when he was fifteen.

When the British-born Gaiman explained to a school advisor that he wanted to write American-style comics, the counselor scoffed and asked if he'd considered accountancy. The experience left Gaiman deeply hurt, the author recalls. The counselor was "the first person to flatly ask me what I wanted to do; and... he told me my goal was unreachable." Gaiman gave up comics for nine years after the experience.

Fortunately, he overcame his disappointment and went on to pen *Sandman*, which, among other honors, won the 1991 World Fantasy Award for Best Short Story, making it the first monthly comic to win a literary prize.

Others may not believe in your dreams, but all that's necessary is that you believe them yourself.

The bee is small among flying creatures, but what it produces is the best of sweet things. (Sirach 11:3)

Help us, Lord, to be willing to trust ourselves even in the face of opposition.

Cutting through Red Tape

In the weeks following September 11, 2001 thousands of people volunteered in and around New York City.

One of those individuals, litigator Jackie Haberfeld, usually earns big bucks in court for her prestigious law firm. But when the call went out for lawyers to donate their time and services to the needy, Haberfeld didn't hesitate. As she explained, "people needed help."

Averaging 30 hours a week at a makeshift office, Haberfeld helped families obtain death certificates in just a few days, a complex process that often takes a few years if a body is missing. Her clients often sought more than legal advice. "Sometimes they just want(ed) you to sit and listen to them," Haberfeld said.

In times of overwhelming trouble and grief, the giving spirit and presence of those eager to help enables us to pull together and move forward, buoyed by the selflessness in everyone.

**Love one another deeply from the heart.
(1 Peter 1:22)**

Give me strength to give something back, dear Savior.

Preserving Appalachian Heritage

With a young generation eager to leave the Appalachian mountain hollows for the big city, some worry that the region's arts and crafts will eventually be lost forever.

Gerry Milnes, folk art curator for the Augusta Heritage Center at Davis and Elkins College in West Virginia, is determined to help preserve and pass on the old traditions.

The center has an apprenticeship program that matches learners with the masters of such arts as headstone carving, hoedown dancing, and Johnboat building.

Financing for the Augusta Center comes primarily from such master workshops for visitors as Dulcimer Week in the spring and the Fiddlers' Reunion in the fall.

Preserving our heritage and sharing it is an important way to influence and enrich the lives of future generations.

The boundary lines have fallen for me in pleasant places; I have a goodly heritage. (Psalm 16:6)

God, help our young people appreciate the past even as they reach toward the future.

Sunny Outlook

At the age of 12, Mattie Stepanek is something of a celebrity. Although he has mitochondrial myopathy, a disease that has already claimed the lives of his three older siblings, he has given great hope to many through his best-selling books of poetry.

He counts former President Jimmy Carter, television talk show host Oprah Winfrey, and comedian and Muscular Dystrophy Association telethon host Jerry Lewis among his friends.

His mother says doctors describe Mattie as living "every day with one foot on the edge of a cliff and the other on a banana peel." He has already well-outlived their expectations.

Yet Mattie Stepanek refuses to waste the time he has fretting about the future. He says, "I just try to live life to the fullest and to remember to play after every storm."

That's good advice. Make time to play after a storm.

Since we are receiving a kingdom that cannot be shaken, let us give thanks. (Hebrews 12:28)

God of all, inspire us to weather life's storms with grace.

A Bridal Bouquet–A Half-Century Late

Bill and Myrtle Williams have run Bill Williams Florist from their Compton, California, home since 1958.

Flowers haven't made them rich, but flowers have made them happy–and this long-time married couple has passed that joy around. If a friend can't afford a bouquet for a special occasion, Bill has been known to give a heavy discount.

Recently, friends of the Williamses learned that the couple's own wedding more than five decades ago had been a very simple affair. Bill had worn work clothes–and there had been no flowers at all. So neighbor and friend Wini Jackson got working. She arranged for donations of a cake, limousine and rings. And on Easter Sunday, the Williamses renewed their wedding vows. Myrtle held a cluster of orchids and roses–her first bridal bouquet.

Seeds of kindness planted for others often yield a bountiful bouquet of love for us.

Clothe yourselves with compassion, kindness, humility, meekness and patience.
(Colossians 3:12)

May we live always, Divine Master, in the knowledge of Your great love.

Potentially Powerful

"Many bright children do not achieve to their abilities," according to Sylvia Rimm, author of *Why Bright Kids Get Poor Grades*. Here are some practical ideas that can help children achieve their full potential:

Have you allowed television to gobble up too much of your family's evenings or weekends? Break that habit.

Is your home or office more cluttered than you'd like? Tame that monster and help youngsters organize their work, too.

Are children getting enough sleep? Try to get everybody to bed an hour earlier.

Come to think of it, most of us could benefit from integrating these habits into our own lives. Remember, when it comes to reaching your potential, age is irrelevant.

Pay attention to how you listen. (Luke 8:18)

Show me where I am falling short, Lord, and lead me to higher ground.

Behind Every Computer

The Army first revealed its electronic numerical integrator and computer, ENIAC, in 1946. John Mauchly and Prespert Eckert received the credit for this new technology. Considered the first electronic computer, ENIAC was originally used to compute ballistics tables. Equations that had previously taken a week to solve were done in seconds.

According to *American Ingenuity,* until ENIAC, ballistics calculations were done by female "computers," working with desktop calculators, pencils and papers.

Those same women took the hardware created by Mauchly and Eckert to solve the equations and configure the tubes and vacuums using only block diagrams and wiring schematics. Their work had always been considered clerical. People were so awed by the hardware that they had never credited the world's first computer programmers and software technicians. Women have been computing from the start.

Who do you know who deserves some recognition?

You are precious in My sight and honored and I love you. (Isaiah 43:3)

Gracious God, urge me to recognize women's as well as men's contributions to the common good.

Choose Your Battles: Advice for Success

Greta Van Susteren, college professor, trial lawyer and host of TV's *On the Record* for Fox News, offers these tips for success:

- Learn from your experiences and move on. Don't waste time or energy blaming others or yourself for setbacks.

- Choose your battles wisely. Some things are worth fighting for; others drain time and energy, and accomplish little.

- Develop good judgment; your knowledge of right and wrong to make choices. Evaluate your motives and reactions.

- Recognize the difference between standing up for yourself and your ideas and being insolent.

- Stretch yourself. Take risks. Try new tactics, career paths.

- Be ready and willing to work hard.

- Know when and where to draw the line. Leave time for family, friends and yourself.

Trust God in all things—and do your best.

Human success is in the hand of the Lord. (Sirach 10:5)

With Your help, Lord, I can face any difficulty, brave any trial.

Olive Oil Wars?

Old versus new. My way. Yours. Is there always only one correct way of doing things?

Moreno Menghini does things the old-fashioned way at his olive press in Asproli, Italy. And it seems local growers prefer his methods, described as "earthy," to what might be called the more sterile ways in nearby Collevalenza. Unwashed olives, leaves and all are put into the press. Said one local, "this isn't oil from the supermarket."

But it is just that product from the more modern and pristine olive press, such as Paolo Scassini's, that attracts many customers including visiting Americans. "From beginning to end," of the process, Scassini said, "these olives are not touched by human hands."

In a world of differences, some things are not a matter of right and wrong, but simply a matter of personal taste.

Who are you to judge your neighbor?
(James 4:12)

Jesus, guide us toward an appreciation of differences.

Make a Life–not Just a Living

Lisa Belkin, author of the "Life's Work" columns in *The New York Times,* wrote about the shift of her own priorities and those of so many others after September 11, 2001.

"All year I have been hearing from friends and strangers who quietly honor the dead by changing the equations of their own lives," she wrote. More beepers are being turned off after hours; more voice mail messages announce without apology that messages won't be checked over weekends. "In all the years I've worked, I've never seen a summer where so many workaholics were gone at once," Belkin noted.

For herself, Belkin admits that for the first time in her working life she too took a *real* vacation in the summer after that fateful September day. "I didn't phone a single office or write a publishable word."

Life can change in an instant–so making a life, not just a living, should be everyone's first priority.

Provoke one another to love and good deeds. (Hebrews 10:24)

With every breath, with every heartbeat, I give You thanks, Father, for Your gift of life and for Your love.

Growing Up on the Job

How early should your child start to work? According to Steve Otfinoski, author of *The Kid's Guide to Money,* the earlier the better. "When you work, you learn many important things...the value of money, how to do a job well and how to deal with other people," he says. He thinks middle school students are ideal candidates for first jobs.

There are many jobs made to order for the young–pet sitting, picking up the mail for vacationing neighbors, mowing lawns, baby sitting.

Once a child begins to earn money then parents can start talking about money management: spending, saving, taxes, charity. Teaching youngsters about work offers an opportunity to encourage punctuality, accuracy and dependability. These are fine tools because they can help create trustworthy, responsible adults.

Growing up is all in a day's work for the young who work.

Train children in the right way. (Proverbs 22:6)

Bless the work of our hands, Master. May all we do give praise to Your name.

Healing Habits

When architectural designer and mother of two young sons Merrie Clark was diagnosed with invasive breast cancer, she began practicing the habits that doctors say may help lead to recovery.

She learned all she could about breast cancer and gathered information on the best local oncologists.

She struggled to keep a positive attitude. Clark fought against stress and fatigue, gave up her college teaching position for the semester, quit her volunteer jobs and spent more time relishing ordinary moments. She relied on her friends to help her sons and husband cope during her treatment and recovery.

Clarke was honest with her doctor because "frank dialogue is the hallmark of a good doctor-patient relationship." And she followed his suggestions, as well as doing everything her treatment required.

Life offers no guarantees, but there is hope and, often, healing.

The Lord created medicines out of the earth, and...by them the physician heals and takes away pain. (Sirach 38:4, 7)

Be with me, Lord, so that I may know Your healing, saving presence this day.

Faith on the Job

In a recent national poll of 500 business leaders, more than half say they've seen unethical actions in their own companies, and 58 percent say competitors have done something unethical to gain an advantage.

Some faith-based groups are now trying to close that gap by helping individuals bring more of their religious values into the workplace.

Rev. Kevin Phillips started and now directs the Business Leadership and Spirituality Network to give executives the opportunity to engage in ethical and spiritual dialogue with peers. Similar groups have sprung up nationwide, offering help in this area not only to senior management but also to young people just starting in business.

"You may be a very religious and moral person at church and with your family," says William Messenger, head of the Boston division of BLSN and an Episcopal priest, "but at work you don't even recognize that what you're facing is an ethical decision."

The next time you're faced with a tough call on the job, ask your conscience, ask your best self.

Act with justice and righteousness.
(Jeremiah 22:3)

Bless my work, Father. May all I do offer You praise.

In the Name of Jesus

After the attacks on the World Trade Center, organizations funneled an enormous amount of financial support to those in need. Those who gave, however, often found it frustrating to watch as people had to jump through hoops and wade through red tape in order to access the funds intended to ease their pain.

Enter Pastor Dave Stone of Louisiana. Backed by an alliance of evangelical churches, Stone went from door-to-door at businesses near Ground Zero. After listening to the hardships experienced by owners and employees, he wrote them checks on the spot. Employees were given $500; business owners received up to several thousand dollars, enough to help with back-rent and other debts.

The money, totaling close to one million dollars, was given with no strings attached. "We wanted to give a cold cup of water in the name of Jesus," said Stone.

There are so many ways to lend a helping hand.

Whoever gives even a cup of cold water...none of these will lose their reward. (Matthew 10:42)

Remind us, Lord, how often You speak through our actions.

Finding the Good in Good-Bye

Saying "good-bye" is one of the most common things we do. In one form or another, we say good-bye virtually everyday.

There is the "C-Ya" at the end of an e-mail, or the "talk to you later" sign-off in a telephone conversation. But some good-byes are bigger than that—like graduations or leaving jobs, like the end of a relationship broken beyond repair, or the death of a parent or friend.

In many languages, the literal meaning of good-bye expresses hope for closeness to God. In English, good-bye is a condensed version of "God be with you."

We should use our good-byes as an opportunity to pray for the people from whom we are taking leave. One of the best ways is with a written note—thanks for the memories; thanks for who you have been to me.

Good-byes can be moments of grace. They change us—and can help us change others.

The Lord bless you and keep you; the Lord make His face to shine upon you, and be gracious to you; the Lord...give you peace. (Numbers 6:24)

Be with me, Lord. Strengthen me with Your love.

A Four-Letter Word for After-School

One fall Ana Veciana-Suarez decided not to register her children in after-school activities. Their only post-class task: **Play!**

The time out came about, in part, because the mother herself was stressed out. "Too frantic to smile, and too exhausted to floss," she recalls. "And the children weren't much better."

The two boys did play—but nobody kept score. "We told stories, and we relaxed," says their mom. And she was able to catch up on her reading and sewing; she even had time to organize her recipes.

"We liked those peaceful evenings so much that we're not rushing back to the way things were," said Ana Veciana-Suarez. "We haven't signed up the boys for anything again this fall, and they're not complaining. Maybe that's because the time off has allowed us to enjoy each other's company."

Sometimes the best times are spent just taking time out to be together.

Be careful then how you live, not as unwise people but as wise, making the most of the time. (Ephesians 5:15)

Slow me down, Lord, that I may not miss You in the times of this day.

Oh My Word!

"You'll never amount to anything," a teacher's deeply disparaging remark, is the very phrase that boxing legend Muhammad Ali claims spurred him on.

Marlo Thomas, author of *The Right Words at the Right Time*, was surprised Ali had carried such negative words around in his head.

"But he didn't let those words defeat him," she observed. "Instead, they pushed Ali to prove her wrong, to go out and achieve." Eventually, Ali brought his Olympic gold medal to the teacher who had uttered those negative words.

"Well, now I'm something," he told her. "I'm the greatest!"

The words which inspired most people Thomas interviewed for her book were, in fact, positive.

"Working on this book has led me to believe that words speak very loudly," Thomas says. "I've discovered how important it is to turn up the volume on the good words in our heads."

Let your speech always be gracious. (Colossians 4:6)

Renewing Healer, help me draw strength even from negative experiences.

Inspiring Robots

The choice of Helen Greiner's future career became clear at the movies.

"Someone did inspire me–R2D2 from *Star Wars*–even though he's not really a person," Greiner recalls. "When I saw that movie–and I was just 11 then–I thought, 'Wow, humans aren't necessarily the only intelligent beings. Wouldn't it be cool if robots really existed'?"

After graduating from MIT, she was one of the three founders of *iRobot*. "We believe robots will eventually help protect people," Greiner explains. "Already we can lower a robot into an oil well where a person could never go. They'll some-day help eliminate land mines. And instead of putting a police officer at risk, we can send a robot to see if a suspect has weapons or if hostages are okay."

Human creativity is stirred in so many ways. Welcome whatever inspires you to do good.

Do all that your mind inclines to.
(1 Samuel 14:7)

I see Your hand in all good things, Creator, and I give praise to Your name.

Faring Well after Welfare

In 1960, Yvonne Rhem-Tittle was a single mother living in the South Bronx on public assistance. She began volunteering to clean bathrooms, iron vestments and answer the telephone to make up for the tuition at St. Augustine's, a local Catholic school, so her kids could attend for free.

Four decades later, Rhem-Tittle is principal at St. Augustine's. Lacking even a high school diploma when she started, the mother of seven children worked her way up from paraprofessional to teacher to principal. She earned her high school and college degrees and a master's degree in education.

What is the most important part of her work these 40 years? "Make children feel special," she observes.

"My mother is a woman who can take adversity and turn it into something positive," says her son Joseph Rhem-Tittle.

His mother's life is a lesson in perseverance and positive thinking. Those are attitudes worth pursuing.

Always persevere. (Ephesians 6:18)

Teach me Your ways, Master, so that I may lead others to You.

Could He Play Quidditch, Too?

If you're a Harry Potter fan, you may be familiar with Nicolas Flamel. In *Harry Potter and the Sorcerer's Stone,* Flamel is the creator of the titular gem, a powerful totem sought by an evil wizard.

What you may not know is that Nicolas Flamel actually existed. A famous alchemist during the Middle Ages, Flamel was rumored to have found the secret of changing lead into gold. Some legends claim he still lives.

In truth, Flamel made a fortune as a professional scribe at a time when many people were unable to read or write. He used that money to create low-incoming housing for the poor, to found free hospitals and to endow churches. Flamel's story is almost as remarkable as the wizardly tales that surround his name.

Fiction often borrows from the real world. Next time you're reading or watching something you suspect might be based on reality, do a little research. You never know what you'll find.

The whole earth is full of His glory. (Isaiah 6:3)

Lord, help us to see the wonder of the world around us.

Parent Based Success

Parents, do you want to help your children succeed in school?

- If your children need tutors, focus on English. That'll help your children understand other subjects, too.
- Talk to your children about your own work or school difficulties so they'll tell you about their problems.
- Tell children stories about the mistakes you or others made when you were their age.
- Encourage your children to participate in music, chess–any non-athletic event. The mind needs exercise as much as, if not more than, the body.
- Limit them to one or two sports.
- Attend parent-teacher conferences.
- Don't rewrite homework for them.
- Be cheerful and positive about life and about your work.

Parents, you, as much as your children's teachers, can never tell where your influence ends.

The Lord honors a father above his children, and He confirms a mother's right over her children. (Sirach 3:2)

Holy Spirit, encourage and inspire parents. Remind them constantly that they are their children's first and most important teachers.

Master Craftsman

When Sam Maloof was in middle school, he took a shop class and never looked back.

For most of his life since, from planks of figured hardwood, chiefly walnut, he has found purpose, satisfaction, beauty and comfort.

At 86, Maloof has achieved a good measure of recognition. The Smithsonian Institute has called him America's most renowned contemporary furniture craftsman, and his rocking chairs have sold for $140,000 at auction.

Los Angeles Times columnist John Balzar admires Maloof, who eschewed the conventional path to success. "He chose not to expand beyond a few shop assistants, and he chose not to franchise his name, even when offered millions to do so," he writes.

"If this is the age when anything is possible," Balzar asks, "isn't it peculiar how narrowly we define the bounds of success?"

What is the measure of your success?

Is not this the carpenter's Son? Is not His mother called Mary? And are not His brothers... And...all His sisters with us?
(Matthew 13:55, 56)

Heavenly Spirit, help me understand true success.

Life off the Balance Beam

Francine Garrett had performed jumps and back flips atop the balance beam perhaps 1,000 times with smooth landings.

But in the winter of 1992, something went terribly wrong. As she stepped off the balance beam, Francine crumpled to the floor. Tearing several ligaments in her left knee in the dismount, Francine had ended her career as a world-class gymnast.

Francine took the discipline and leadership skills she had learned as an athlete, matched them with a background in biology, and began a new career–in medical school. By the time she was a sixth-year medical student at Albert Einstein College of Medicine of Yeshiva University in the Bronx, she had become a student-mentor. She is a coach now, helping new students, especially minorities, negotiate the rigors of their training.

Although the transition from gymnastics to medicine was jolting, Francine says: "I'm happy now. I love mentoring. It's exciting to help them toward their goals."

What knowledge can you pass along?

Teach what is good. (Titus 2:3)

Guide me, Master, that I may know Your will.

Coping with Terrible Realities

In the aftermath of the September 11th terrorist attacks in America, people had a variety of reactions.

Scott Russell Sanders, a writer and educator, said that he didn't feel fear or outrage so much as "a soul-deep sorrow."

Now as never before, Sanders said he experienced "the pain of all people who suffer from cruelty or hostility or neglect. It was as though a layer of skin had been peeled away from my nerves.

"In this darkness of shared pain I saw that suffering, unattended, breeds cruelty, which breeds more suffering. And I realized as never before that our task as humans is to reduce the load of pain in the world, to alleviate suffering in everyone we meet, in every way we can."

That's a tall order. But Sanders and others feel strongly that there is no better way to a lasting peace. What do you think?

**Speak the truth to one another, render...judgments that are true and make for peace, do not devise evil...love no false oath.
(Zechariah 8:16-17)**

Jesus, help me to find ways to promote peace.

Teaching–and Singing a Song

Michael Ortner took time off from his job in Virginia to volunteer in Kenya in Africa. At the end of his trip, he visited a local elementary school.

There he found classrooms with no teachers and with students seated two or three at one desk, teaching themselves with the use of old materials. The principal handed him chalk, asking that he teach math, science and geography for the next two hours. "My teaching experience amounted to zero, but these were some of my favorite subjects," Ortner says.

Two hours flew by–and the students thanked their visiting teacher by singing him a song and asking that he return the favor. "I could only think of a Kenny Rogers song," he recalls. "So now there exists in Kenya a village where 40 children know the words to 'The Gambler.'"

"I only wish more teachers could spend time with kids who want to learn as much as these kids do," Ortner said.

Teaching and learning are bound together. Respect both.

Teach the way of God. (Matthew 22:16)

Teach me Your ways, Lord, that I may know the way to bring others to You.

Great Movies, Great Themes

Many people *know* the importance of social justice, but really don't think much about it.

So Patrick McCormick, a Christian ethics professor, wrote in *U.S. Catholic* about several classic films that raise serious issues. *The Grapes of Wrath,* based on John Steinbeck's novel "is *the* American film about poverty, class, and the struggle for economic justice."

It's a Wonderful Life features an extraordinary, ordinary hero who frustrates the machinations of a greedy banker and helps create "a vibrant community of friends and neighbors." Set in a cotton mill, *Norma Rae* "offers a reinvigorated vision of unions...and it acknowledges that women are workers, too." Finally, *Dead Man Walking* is the "film version of Sister Helen Prejean's account of her death row ministry" including her "conflicting moral duties to the killer and his victim's families."

Take the time to consider responsibilities to neighbors, especially those in greatest need of simple justice.

Do not be hard-hearted or tight-fisted toward your needy neighbor. (Deuteronomy 15:7)

Christ, open our hearts to the deepest concerns of all our brothers and sisters. Then help us actively support them.

Like Grandfather, Like Grandson

Rajmohan Gandhi was a teenager when he saw his grandfather, Mohandas Mahatma Gandhi, lead India's nonviolent liberation from Great Britain and when the elder Gandhi was assassinated in 1948.

Rajmohan Gandhi often reflects on the message of his grandfather's life for today's world. "My grandfather was a great champion of reconciliation. When people try peacefully to work out their problems with each other, not only is it a powerful force for good, but this example becomes a model for others trying to do the same."

All change begins with individuals, he believes. "In the Koran there is a wonderful verse: 'Even God will not change a society, unless the people of the society change themselves.' I think Hindus, Christians, Jews and Muslims should reflect on that profound truth. Then one day we may all see my grandfather's vision of a better world."

For a better world, start by changing yourself.

Pray that you may not come into the time of trial. (Matthew 26:41)

Grant us Your peace, Master. May we live each day in hope.

Transplanting Life

The first time that Chantyl Peterson met New York City firefighter Terry Farrell she was six. She rode his fire truck and ate lunch with him and some of his friends at the World Trade Center in New York City.

Prior to that joyous trip, the Nevada child had been diagnosed with aplastic anemia, a disease that stops the functions of bone marrow. Family members weren't a match for a bone marrow transplant, but Farrell, who had signed up with the National Marrow Donor Program Registry, was. His donation saved her life. Chantyl and her folks made that visit to thank him.

On September 11, 2001, the now teenage Chantyl watched television reports of the destruction of the Twin Towers and she worried about Farrell. Like many other firefighters, Farrell died. Chantyl made another visit to New York for Farrell's funeral.

Yet, even in death, in Chantyl's every breath, the generous firefighter lives on.

Honor those who give of themselves.

In the memory of virtue is immortality.
(Wisdom of Solomon 4:1)

With every breath, I praise You, Father. You are the source of life and all good things.

Peace to a City in Pain

In the days following the attacks of September 11, 2001, a brother and sister fashioned a *Sukkah* in a lot behind his Brooklyn loft (apartment). These temporary dwellings are meant to be places in which to rejoice during the Jewish harvest festival of Sukkoth. But they are also reminders of "the impermanence of all structures and the uncertainty of the harvest."

"And that," said Samantha M. Shapiro, writing in *The New York Times*, "in light of what had happened across the East River in Manhattan seemed particularly resonant."

Sukkah speaks to the truth that any building at any moment could fall; that indeed we continually dwell with uncertainty. Yet we pray that God will "spread a Sukkah of peace over us."

So even though the harvest is a distant reality, the prayer of Sukkah has meaning for all of us. Amidst life's uncertainties may the Holy One give us His comfort!

Our days pass away...our years come to an end like a sigh. The days of our life are seventy years, or perhaps eighty, if we are strong. (Psalm 90:9-10)

God our King, remind me that life here is a prelude to life eternal under the shadow of Your wings.

Get Your Motor Runnin'

Butler, Wisconsin, has been home to what some might consider to be an odd tradition. Each fall, a flatbed truck loaded with food donations and escorted by 20 to 30 motorcyclists pulls up to St. Agnes Church, where the Milwaukee-area bikers unload their donations and stock the St. Agnes food pantry. The delivery is followed by raffles and other fundraising to support the pantry, which in turn assists about 20 families a month.

According to bikers involved with the food drive, the tradition grew out of a desire to return a favor; 20 years ago, a few of the bikers and their families had turned to the food pantry for assistance during hard times. The first food drive was a way to say "thank you."

An act of kindness can bring returns from the most unexpected places. By helping others, you may be sparking good deeds you don't even realize.

See what almsgiving accomplishes. (Tobit 14:11)

Lord, help us to set an example for others.

Ya Just Missed 'Em...

Saul Eiser was visiting his father at work when he was sent to a local hotel coffee shop to pick up lunch.

At the shop, Saul was shocked—Babe Ruth, the legendary baseball player, sat at a table with some companions. Saul, not having a pen or paper, ran back to his father's office to retrieve those necessary items and returned to the coffee shop.

Saul nervously approached "The Babe" and asked for his autograph. "Sure, kid," Ruth responded, adding, "You shoulda been here five minutes earlier, kid. You coulda got Ty Cobb and Tris Speaker, too."

Saul might have missed the opportunity to meet those other famous ballplayers, but he *did* wind up with Ruth's autograph and a story worth telling for the rest of his life.

Greet life's twists and turns with a little humor and you'll be surprised how just about any situation can turn out positive.

Hope does not disappoint us. (Romans 5:5)

Lord, help us to laugh at life's twists and turns.

Rescue Mission

Pia grew up in the slums of Manila in the Philippines, in her grandmother's house–"a house without love," by her description. "I can only remember shoutings and beatings," she recalls.

Soon, Pia was living on the streets; by 12, she had become a victim of psychological and physical abuse in the child-sex industry. That's when she met Rev. Shay Cullen, an Irish Catholic missionary. "He rescued me," she says. As director of the PREDA Child Protection Center, he developed a rehabilitation program that helped Pia and other young girls like her.

With his help, Pia found hope. Today, she works with Rev. Cullen to protect children's rights in her homeland–offering the hope she found to other girls who find themselves on the streets. Pia even wants to be a police officer so she can be on the frontline of that battle.

With love and caring, the rescued is today the rescuer. Even in the darkness, there is always the light of hope.

The disciple took her into his own home. (John 19:27)

Be with me, Lord. Help me see Your light in the darkness of this day.

David vs. Goliath in Medicine

Some would categorize Western medicine, with its scientific method and pharmaceutical connections, as a Goliath to holistic medicine's David.

The same mismatch apparently also exists in the world of animal medicine. A veterinarian writing in *Bark* magazine tells of the successful treatment of a dog with seizures using alternative medicine.

Originally the owner went the conventional route, giving the pet prescribed medications that didn't work and caused terrible side effects. Then a six-month regimen of homemade food, vitamins, herbs and acupuncture returned the dog to good health.

More and more of us seem to be turning to some forms of alternative healing, while not abandoning traditional Western medicine with its benefits.

Rather than a pitched battle, what makes most sense might be to keep an open mind and to keep learning about the best ways to health – for yourself, your loved ones and your four-footed companions, as well.

Glorify God in your body. (1 Corinthians 6:20)

Divine Healer, comfort us in times of distress.

Fighting Against Fear

When terrorists blew up Carmen Gurruchaga's apartment, it was the latest in an intensifying campaign of attacks against the journalist. Basque separatists had already organized smear campaigns against Gurruchaga and had even firebombed her office at the Spanish newspaper, *El Mundo*.

Yet Gurruchaga continues to report, as she has since 1981, about the organization that has killed more than 800 people in the last three decades, including one of her co-workers. She does take precautions though–she's moved out of the region and now travels with armed guards. "I am conscious of the risk I run, but fear leads nowhere," Gurruchaga says. "I'm going to fight in whatever way I can, even if it's only with a pen and paper."

Few worthwhile things are without risk. Have the courage to fight for what is right, to speak out for truth and for justice.

Speak out for those who cannot speak, for the rights of all the destitute. ...Defend the rights of the poor and needy. (Proverbs 31:8-9)

Help us, Lord, to understand where we can make change and help us to have the courage to do so.

Stop Wasting Water

Water is always a precious necessity. Here are a few tips for saving water at home:

1. Don't run the water while brushing your teeth. You can waste up to four gallons.

2. Flush one fewer time each day. If everyone in the United Sates did that, it would save nearly a billion gallons of water every day.

3. Use a car wash. They recycle anywhere from 30 to 90 percent of the water used.

4. Thaw frozen foods in the refrigerator rather than under running water.

5. Fix steam leaks, dripping faucets, leaky pipes.

Water is a finite but life-sustaining resource. Conserve it.

> **You visit the earth and water it...the river of God is full of water...You water its furrows abundantly...softening it with showers. (Psalm 65:9, 10)**

Inspire us to find ways to preserve our precious resources, Holy Spirit.

The Winning Ticket

Emily Koper, determined to buy a mountain bike, had been saving her allowance all year. Her father Ed, who owned several bikes, offered her any of them, but Emily wanted a brand new one.

One day, as Christmas neared and Emily and her dad shopped, they met a Salvation Army volunteer. "Can we give something?" Emily asked her dad. "Sorry," he replied, "but I'm out of change."

Not long after that, Emily decided to hand her $58 savings to the Salvation Army to help the poor. Inspired by her actions, her father donated two bikes to a car dealer collecting used bikes for poor children. In return he received two tickets for a chance to win a 21-speed bike.

The second ticket proved to be the winner and Emily had her bike after all.

Few of our charitable actions will meet with a return in quite this way, but the fact is, in giving, we do receive.

He gave alms generously. (Acts 10:2)

Praise to You Father for the goodness and beauty You offer me every day.

The Eye Exam that Saved His Life

Michael Lomonaco, the top chef at the World Trade Center's Windows on the World restaurant, normally arrived at his 106th-floor kitchen at 8:15 each morning. But on September 11, 2001, he decided to first go for an eye exam.

His change of plans saved his life, as a terrorist attack on the World Trade Center that morning killed thousands, including more than seventy of his co-workers.

Lomonaco talks often of that Tuesday's events. "When I looked up, I thought immediately of my co-workers, my colleagues, my friends," he recalls. "While the heart and the wounds of loss might heal, the loss will always be there. ...Who is not changed forever?"

One day, Lomonaco hopes to cook in a New York restaurant with other survivors from Windows on the World. "I'd like to bring that family together again," he says.

Some moments change our lives forever. Do all you can to see that they are changed for the better.

Do not give your heart to grief...you do the dead no good, and you injure yourself. (Sirach 38: 20, 21)

Father, shelter me in the warmth of Your comforting and strengthening love.

The Daily Juggling Act

Let's face it: anyone with a full-time job and full-time family responsibilities is living a stressful life. But recent studies have shown that "role jugglers" are less likely to be anxious or depressed, or have stress-related health problems.

Managing multiple roles? Try the following to make juggling work for you:

- Focus on one place and one thing at a time. Think about work at work, and focus on the family at home.

- Accentuate the positive. Appreciate the variety of all you do.

- Lighten your load. If work is too much, talk to the boss; if home is getting too hectic, discuss divvying up the chores.

One other tip: Get away from your desk and enjoy lunch with your colleagues or take a little walk.

When you feel the balancing act starting to teeter, it never hurts to offer a prayer. The Lord is never too stressed out to listen.

Cast your burden on the Lord, and He will sustain you. (Psalm 55:22)

Be with me, Holy One, at work and at home.

A Way Out of Poverty: Books

"Working in the fields or working on textiles is hard. We do not want our children to live this way. We want them to have a better life so their life will not be as hard as ours," said Victoria Xinico.

Other Guatemalan parents are also committed to their children's education as a way out of subsistence farming. But providing the tools for learning is hard too. The Berninger brothers, Jeff and Joe, realized that one way was to get textbooks to eager students.

They began the Ohio-based Cooperative for Education to find sponsors such as Rotary International to donate money for book programs and other educational initiatives. The Guatemalan parents also make a financial investment according to their ability.

The brothers' reward is seeing the joy and hopefulness that books bring.

There are many forms of literacy. To give the gift of literacy to another, child or adult, is a precious gift.

He went to the synagogue on the Sabbath day, as was His custom. (Jesus) stood up to read. (Luke 4:16)

Nurture in us an appreciation for education, Jesus.

Discovering the Discoverer

It's common knowledge that Christopher Columbus set out on his famous voyage to prove that the world was round. His crew, largely composed of criminals, made a storm-wracked voyage that cost the lives of numerous starving sailors. Years later, Columbus died in a Spanish prison, penniless, disgraced and suffering from syphilis. Right?

Wrong. All these stories are common myths surrounding the life of the famed explorer. For the record, Columbus, like most well-learned men of the time, knew the Earth was spherical. The 1492 voyage to the New World was made under almost ideal conditions and no one from the crew of mostly professional sailors died. Columbus himself passed away at the age of 55 in his own apartment, attended by family and friends. He suffered only from gout and declining eyesight.

Sometimes even "common knowledge" is a little lax on the knowledge aspect. Dig deeper— you'll be surprised at what you find.

Speak the truth to one another.
(Zechariah 8:16)

Lord, please help us to always quest for knowledge and understanding.

New Life Begets New Life

When Jennifer Rogers' daughter announced that she and her husband were expecting twins, the grandmother-to-be decided to draw them a family tree.

"The project quickly became a confusing tangle of broken lines and empty boxes," she says. "Divorce, remarriage and adoption have turned us into the sort of larger 'blended' clan that is increasingly the norm in American society."

Ultimately, Rogers designed a scrapbook called *Welcome-to-the-Family Field Book and Survival Guide*. She sent surveys to relatives far and wide, devoting a page in the scrapbook to each person. She then assembled the responses, adding photographs and newspaper clippings.

"In searching to define ourselves, we discovered things we had never known about one another," Rogers says. "We grew exuberant. Old fractures healed. The book we created together became more than the sum of its parts."

How can you bring your family members closer together?

Whose offspring are worthy of honor? Human offspring. (Sirach 10:19)

Show us new ways to appreciate the gift of family, Lord.

"Prima Donna" Men Have Named You

When Jay Livingston first penned the lyrics to the classic "Mona Lisa," it was called, "Prima Donna." Luckily, Wyn, the wife of Livingston's songwriting partner Ray Evans, thought that "Mona Lisa" sounded nicer.

Livingston started a dance band in the 1930s and became friendly with musician Evans. In 1944, legendary songwriter Johnny Mercer summoned them to Hollywood. They had their heyday in the 1940s and 1950s with songs like "Buttons and Bows," "Tammy," "Que Será, Será," and "Silver Bells." They turned out songs for more than 80 movies, including three Academy Award winners.

Livingston and Hughes ended their careers composing theme music for such television series as "Bonanza" and "Mr. Ed." In fact, it's Livingston chanting the famous lines: "a horse is a horse, of course, of course."

Most of our work will not win awards. But it will always have the potential to make the world a more humane place.

Commit your work to the Lord. (Proverbs 16:3)

I sing Your praises, Master, for You have given me life and every good thing.

Making a Difference

For decades, a mountain in the Adirondacks has been unofficially known as Goodman Mountain because the Goodman family from New York City had a cottage there.

In 1964, Andrew Goodman, Michael Schwerner and James Chaney joined a voter registration campaign in Mississippi. At the end of their first day they were detained by a sheriff's deputy and killed for trying to enfranchise Black Mississippians.

Bill Frenette, an historian from Tupper Lake, New York, wants to commemorate Goodman's life and sacrifice by having the nearby mountain officially named in his honor.

Says Frenette, "I would like to think people will look at it and say, 'That's Goodman Mountain', ...the mountain loved by a wealthy kid who gave up his life to help people in Mississippi."

Let us remember those who have given their lives in the service of others. Let us all serve in our own way.

**Remember the word that I said to you.
(John 15:20)**

Father, remind us to celebrate the lives and deeds of those who have lived and died for equal justice under the law for all.

Someone To Lean On

Tom Brady, the young quarterback who led the New England Patriots to a Super Bowl victory in 2002, gives all the credit for his success to his parents, Tom Sr. and Galynn. In fact, though Brady doesn't get to see them or his three older sisters as often as he'd like, their relationship has never been stronger.

Brady's mom was a nurturer who kept her children grounded, while his dad worked long hours to support his family but still found time to toss a football with his son. "He was able to grow his wings," says Tom, Sr., "and that is what it's all about."

That is indeed the truth when it comes to parents and children. Love them, hold them, be someone to lean on, yet give them their wings and let them fly.

Parenting can, at times, be the toughest job in the world, but it sure makes it all worthwhile when a son like Tom Brady says, "They are the reason I am what I am today."

Your Father in heaven (will) give good things to those who ask Him. (Matthew 7:11)

Father, help parents to nurture and then let go.

Bowery Mission

Life on "The Bowery."

For many, the words conjure images of homeless, unkempt, men and women whose drinking and/or drug use is out of control.

But at the Bowery Mission, founded in 1879 in New York City, there is another perspective. The mission provides shelter, services and food for body and soul to God's children.

In the past, attendance at services was mandatory. Nowadays there is still preaching, singing and Scripture reading, but emphasis is on presenting testimony from people who have recovered.

"I wanted to be part of the beauty of this place," said James Macklin, who went there in the 1980s after cocaine addiction overwhelmed his life. Today he is their director of outreach.

The warmth of staff and volunteers reminds the people who go there that they're not hopeless cases. Instead, the message conveyed, said one pastor, is that "we love you. We take you seriously."

Be merciful, just as your Father is merciful. (Luke 6:36)

Help us, Lord, to find ways to make others feel welcome.

Legacy of Century-Old Eyes

When Manuel Alvarez Bravo died at the age of 100 in October 2002, he left behind images that captured the heart and soul of his native Mexico.

Arguably that nation's greatest photographer and a world master of his art, Bravo was a leader in an artistic revolution that flowered after the Revolution of 1910-21. His photography combined artistic influences from abroad with a profoundly Mexican subject matter. There are images of urban life as well of the countryside. Growing up in the midst of revolutionary violence that claimed a million lives, many of those images also include death, either explicitly or implicitly.

And how did Bravo start on the road to seeing life through the lens? He learned the basics of photography from a family friend who gave him a camera bought at a pawnshop.

Keep your eyes open to the world and wonder around you.

I do hope to see you. (Romans 15:24)

Today grant that I may see Your face in those around me, Lord.

Helping the Uninsured

At a Charlottesville, Virginia, chemotherapy lab one morning, breast-cancer patient Sarah Terry met first time patient Teri Mullins. Mullins was uninsured.

Soon after, Terry, a Chamber of Commerce executive director, spoke to newspaper editor Ken Woodley about Mullins's plight. Woodley came up with an idea: put a box on state tax returns to be checked off by taxpayers contributing to uninsured patients with grave illnesses.

Terry used her connections to lobby state legislators and the Uninsured Medical Catastrophe Fund was soon signed into law. It has become a success story.

Meanwhile, thanks to a fellow cancer survivor and the fund, Teri Mullins had a life-saving mastectomy. As an appreciative Mullins said, "Life shouldn't be based on how fat your wallet is."

In helping one person, many more can be touched.

Be rich in good works, generous.
(1 Timothy 6:18)

When someone is in need, I will rise to fill it, Holy Giver.

Building Understanding

Religion doesn't have to be the arena for major conflict and misunderstanding that it often is. Some educators are trying to build bridges of understanding through efforts such as the Catholic/ Jewish Education Enrichment Program.

"Having a rabbi come to class gives the students the opportunity to see that we're bridging cultures, and that's part of what this class is about," said religion teacher Edward Finch of Chicago's Resurrection High School. "It's important for both communities to...know each other. We learn more about ourselves the more we learn about others."

Rabbi Larry Edwards said the program began as the result of a friendship between a rabbi and a priest. "It continues to be very much about building relationships," he says.

Said another rabbi, "When people who are different are friends with each other, only then is God happy."

(Jesus) answered, "It is written, 'One does not live by bread alone'." (Matthew 4:4)

May we use the gift of faith to bring us together, Father.

Running to Stay on Track

Three years after coming to grips with alcoholism, Molly Barker, a triathlete who competes in "Ironman" competitions and the mother of two children, founded Girls on the Run. This is an after-school program that uses running to boost girls' self-esteem.

"I just thought, 'Wouldn't it be neat if I could give young women the same feeling I have when I get out there and run'?"

In the programs, girls participate in activities designed to promote self-awareness, relationship skills and positive body image, while training and eventually running a 5K (3.1 mile) race. "What matters is how they encourage their teammates," Barker says

Barker believes that everything she's gone through led her to found GOTR. "Once I got sober I knew I had to find a calling," she says. "The emptiness I used to feel is now filled."

Finding "something that matters" is always worth the pain of discovery.

I determined to take (Wisdom) to live with me, knowing that she would give me good counsel and encouragement in cares and grief. (Wisdom of Solomon 8:9)

What is the meaning of my life, Creator God?

Shut Out Worry

Sir William Osler was a renowned Canadian physician and professor of medicine in the late 19th and early 20th centuries. He promoted high professional standards, insisting that medical students have vital responsibilities to patients. He also knew that severe anxiety was detrimental to their lives and work.

Once, aboard an ocean liner, the captain showed him how watertight compartments keep the ship afloat in case of a major leak. The doctor later told his medical students: "Each of you is much more marvelous than that great liner and bound on a far longer voyage. Learn to master your life by living each day in a day-tight compartment. ...Touch a button and hear the iron doors shutting out the past–the dead yesterdays. Touch another and shut off the future–the unborn tomorrows. Then you are safe–safe for today."

Worry can drown us if we let it flow unchecked. Instead, do the best you can and trust in God to keep you safe.

It was You who took me from the womb; You kept me safe on my mother's breast...and since my mother bore me You have been my God. (Psalm 22:9,10)

Holy God, calm my fears and take my troubles. You are my beginning, my end, my all.

In the Name of Laura

Unfathomable as it seems, 2,000 children are reported missing in the U.S. every day. Five years ago, 12-year-old Laura Smither became one of them.

Two weeks after her disappearance, Laura was found dead. Though her parents, Bob and Gay Smither, were devastated, they were also inspired by the manner in which the people in their Texas town came together to search for their daughter.

The Smithers founded the Laura Recovery Center Foundation, which has turned the search for missing children into a science. Since its inception a year after Laura's disappearance, the Foundation has provided assistance to families in 446 missing-person cases. It developed a manual that has become a guide for families and communities in shock and distress.

The Smithers have tried to help others, like themselves, who must deal with unspeakable tragedy. Actions like theirs, and prayer, can help heal the heart's deepest wounds.

Overcome evil with good. (Romans 12:21)

Savior, help me to see and bring out the best in people.

Yum, A Chocolate Factory

Needing a change, Jacques Torres, former executive pastry chef at LeCirque 2000, left that top rated restaurant. He opened a chocolate factory and retail store in Brooklyn with his partners.

Owning a business requires long hours, but– "You can say 'apple' in front of people, or 'pear,' but if you say 'chocolate'–it's a magic ingredient," said Torres. "It has the same compound your brain produces when in love. That perhaps helps people to eat chocolate. It is a mood elevator."

Chocolate *is* big business. The Chocolate Manufacturers Association, a trade group, estimates retailers sell more than $13 billion worth annually.

The chocolate factory workers are happy with what they do and they bring happiness to others. What more can you ask for in a job? ...Do you ask of your job? ...Do you bring to it?

There is nothing better for mortals than to eat and drink, and find enjoyment in their toil. (Ecclesiastes 2:24)

Let us find happiness and share it with others, Jesus.

The Write Stuff

On her son's first birthday, Marie Detter wrote him a letter. Sealing it in an envelope, she tucked it away until Jared grew up.

She did the same for each birthday. Marie's husband Al had a hard time understanding the point of this exercise. "Nice idea," he thought, "but that's a lot of work. We'll always remember these moments anyway so why bother?"

After marrying and moving with his wife into their own home, Jared received his letters. The next time his parents came for a visit, he shared the prized notes with them.

Jared's father was stunned. "Up until that time, they were just 18 nice letters written to my son by my wife," he said. "Now they were priceless treasures that would belong to the entire family."

How many different ways could this type of gift be shared? Find a half-hour and write a letter to a friend or family member.

Time will bless and multiply your thoughtfulness.

I decided, after investigating everything carefully...to write an orderly account for you. (Luke 1:3)

Show us new ways to appreciate each other, Spirit of Love.

Building for the Future

"We have a great name," says Dr. Mustapha Abady, professor of classical studies at the University of Alexandria. "The challenge is living up to it."

Abady was referring to the Library of Alexandria, which was preparing for its grand opening. The institution's reputation stretches back to 300 B.C., when scholars came to Alexandria to use its more than 700,000 scrolls.

Today's 31,000-square-foot building, designed to hold four million books, has a collection of just a few hundred thousand volumes. Director Ismail Serageldin's plan is to develop world-class collections in three areas: the ancient library itself, Alexandria and Egypt.

Like the new Library at Alexandria, your life is built on a strong foundation. Concentrate on developing the gifts you have been given by our Creator. Live up to them.

To all those who have, more will be given...but from those who have nothing, even what they have will be taken away. (Matthew 25:29)

Help me use my resources wisely, O God.

A Baseball Pioneer

Suzyn Waldman had waited her whole life for the opportunity, and even breast cancer wasn't going to stop her from doing what she believed she was always meant to do.

So in the spring of 1996, the former musical theater actress stepped into the New York Yankees broadcasting booth and into the record books. She was the first woman hired to do play-by-play coverage for a Major League team.

Before each telecast, Waldman carefully covered her bald head with a wig. She endured chemotherapy without complaint and went about doing her job. The way she saw it, "They were going to have to kill me to keep me out of the booth."

Today, Waldman is very much alive and well, and cancer free. She is also the pre- and post- game reporter for the Yankees on the YES Network.

Everyone has some suffering to overcome and some opportunity to turn into achievement – if we have courage and hope.

Be courageous. (2 Samuel 13:28)

Assist me in finding what I'm meant to do, Lord Savior.

Planting Hope

Ann's past week had been bad followed by worse. Work included one battle after another. On the home front, she seemed constantly at odds with both her mother and husband.

On this Sunday afternoon, all Ann wanted was to turn on her television–and turn off the world.

But Ann's three-year-old Hannah had other plans.

"Let's go do the garden, mommy. Please! You promised!" she chanted repeatedly–until Ann surrendered.

Once outside in the crisp fall air, mother and daughter began raking leaves. Clearing one section of the garden, Ann dug holes and Hannah dropped in tulip and crocus bulbs that had been sitting forgotten on Ann's shelf for weeks.

Hours passed by–and laughter and fun filled each one. "Isn't it easier when I help?" Hannah asked her mother as they returned to the house.

"More than you'll ever know," Ann said, as her week of big problems faded away in her little child's arms.

Hope does not disappoint us. (Romans 5:5)l

Even in my darkest hour, Master, You send Your light to lead me home.

Business As Usual?

Everyone has heard tales of how competitive and cutthroat corporate culture can be.

Rev. Steve Lawler, an Episcopal priest and St. Louis-based ethics consultant, tells of a young manager at a marketing communications firm who, after being fired, was besieged by a co-worker who wanted the designer chair, size tall, in which the now-former manager was sitting.

At the same time, another executive tried to stake a claim to the popular chair by putting his coffee mug and some files in the office.

That's a reminder that at a time when corporate governance is seriously deficient, the individual is most important. And the actions of every person should be "something like the golden rule," says Rev. Lawler.

Do you practice the golden rule on the job, in the office, at home, in shops, everywhere?

In everything do to others as you would have them do to you; for this is the Law and the Prophets. (Matthew 7:12)

Help me have the courage to speak out against wrongdoing in the workplace, Lord.

In Family, We Find Strength

Talavera mansion has overlooked the majestic Catskills and Berkshires since 1807. Once owners of 294 acres, the Van Ness and Philip families' land holdings have diminished to 125 acres. Labor, machinery and other costs to maintain the property and orchards and remain competitive nearly caused the family to lose the farm and orchards.

The five Philip siblings, all of whom pursue varied professions, and their mother banded together to save the land so long connected to their family history.

As nearby orchards went out of business, the Philip's modernized their operations. Now, every fall, thousands of visitors descend upon the mansion, where the Philip family, descendents of the original owners, run a pick-your-own apple orchard. Macintosh, Mutsu, and Jonagolds abound.

There are few challenges a family can't overcome together.

Honor your father and your mother. (Mark 7:10)

God, help me love my family in good times and bad.

More than an Apple for the Teacher

Most of us have had favorite teachers. For Kate Knowles, there was Sister Frances Mary who taught eighth grade at St. Mary's School in Sterling, Illinois.

Sister Frances Mary was the first to ask Knowles' opinions and listen to them. She introduced Knowles to literature and poetry, encouraging her to write her first short story.

"When I became a teacher myself I drew especially on my memories of Sister Frances Mary to keep aware of my potential for affecting students' lives," she said.

So when Knowles met a former student of her own who said, "You are the best teacher I ever had," she decided to find her own "best teacher" and say, "Thanks!" as well.

It took a little detective work, but in time they had a reunion and developed a warm friendship.

Wherever lessons are taught they should be offered in love and accepted with thanks.

A disciple is not above the teacher, but everyone who is fully qualified will be like the teacher. (Luke 6:39)

Teach me Your ways, Master. Guide me in all I do this day.

Getting Out of the Fast Lane

Do you eat while you work, drive, or sit at the computer? Is it hard to remember when you laughed last? Are you always rushed? If you answered, "Yes," it's time to cruise for a while in the slow lane.

Jesus understood the need to slip away. Busy teaching God's word, traveling and healing, He also rested, spending time alone with God in prayer; finding time to enjoy celebrations with family and friends. So too in our lives. There is the need to consciously slow down and schedule time for yourself, your spouse, your family and friends.

"Whenever I slip out of the fast lane, I find that God, family and friends are waiting to show me the life I'm speeding past," said Kathryn Lay in *Catholic Digest*. "There are many things to see and do in the slow lane...with joy."

Slow down for your own sake–and for God's.

In returning and rest you shall be saved; in quietness and in trust shall be your strength. (Isaiah 30:15)

Remind us that in all times and seasons, You are with us, Master, offering us hope and sending us Your love.

Finding a Good Egg

Every year *Catholic Digest* invites readers to nominate unsung heroes among us–those quiet "Good Eggs" of the world who do good deeds simply because good deeds need to be done.

Recent winners include octogenarian Paul Stringham, a physician and father of five adopted children. He started a Doctor's Free Clinic in his hometown of St. George, Utah. At the clinic, doctors volunteer their services to people who otherwise would be without medical care.

"Good Egg" Anne Marie Bonaime of Walhalla, North Dakota opened her home to neighbors when devastating floods in the upper Midwest forced many to evacuate their own houses. She also volunteers at her parish church. "Whenever there is a need, Anne Marie is there," says her friend Judy Beaudrie. "She just gives of herself quietly."

If we think for a minute, each of us knows a "good egg"–someone who truly does make our world a better place.

As you did it to one of the least...members of My family, you did it to Me. (Matthew 25:40)

I give thanks, Father, for the people this day who will show me Your love.

The Primary Voter

Now here's a man who took voting seriously. Neil Tillotson, a New Hampshire industrialist who lived to the age of 102, was so inspired as a teenager by a speech by Teddy Roosevelt that decades later he put Dixville Notch on the map as a polling place.

After buying a resort hotel in Dixville Notch, Tillotson learned that the nearest polling place was 50 miles away. He had the town incorporated for voting purposes. As the town moderator, Tillotson was always the first to place his vote in the ballot box.

Since the 1960s, the polls at Dixville Notch have opened at midnight for New Hampshire's first-in-the-nation primary and election days. Because of the hoopla surrounding the early votes, presidential hopefuls often stop there while on the campaign trail.

There is nothing more integral to our nation than participatory democracy. Voting is both a privilege and a right; one we should take seriously. Vote!

Do nothing without deliberation, but when you have acted, do not regret it. (Sirach 32:19)

Thank you for blessings of liberty, Lord of the nations.

Laughing at Death

When someone in Sapanta, Romania dies, a special carving marks his or her grave in the Merry Cemetery, next to the Church of the Assumption.

Farmer and poet Dumitru Pop creates a poetic and pictorial homage to the deceased resident on oaken grave markers. The cemetery has hundreds of colorfully painted carvings showing people in life or at the moment of death.

The epitaphs, said to be messages from the deceased, are inspired by routine events in their lives. Some are humorous commentaries on their all-too-human weaknesses.

Laughing at death is something these Romanians seem to have acquired from their Dacian ancestors, fearless fighters who died believing they'd meet their supreme god Zalmoxis.

Rev. Grigore Lutai, the town's Orthodox priest says residents "don't react to death as though it were a tragedy. Death is just a passage to another life."

That's a good reminder for each of us.

Where, O death, is your victory? Where, O death, is your sting? ...thanks be to God, who gives us the victory through our Lord Jesus Christ. (1 Corinthians 15:55,57)

Jesus, Merciful Savior, comfort the dying and assure them of Your victory over death.

Strengthen Your Body's Immunity

Science tells us that it is possible to boost our immunity, but we're the only ones who can make the necessary changes in our lives. Health writer Michael Castleman offers these tips:

1. Eat foods rich in fiber and antioxidants—fruits, vegetables, whole grains, nuts.

2. Take a multiple vitamin-mineral supplement.

3. Nurture your social relationships.

4. Exercise regularly.

5. Be vaccinated against infectious disease.

6. Get enough sleep.

7. Don't smoke.

8. Relax deeply. Stress reduces immune function.

9. Laugh. It provides a light whole-body exercise easing muscle tension and anxiety.

Good health adds to your enjoyment of life. Be gentle with yourself while you develop positive habits.

There is no wealth better than health of body, and no gladness above joy of heart. (Sirach 30:16)

May I always appreciate Your gift of good health, Lord.

Give Us This Day Our Daily Brew

The monks of Belgium's Westmalle Monastery are members of one of Roman Catholicism's strictest, most secluded religious orders. These Trappist monks spend their lives behind monastery walls, ascetic, silent and seemingly a world away from the rest of us.

But even they must earn their daily bread. So when not at prayer, these Trappists and those of five other Belgian monasteries brew world-class beer selling for $11 to $17 a bottle.

"The monks are able to put things in perspective," says Marlene Hurdak, director of public relations for the brewery. "They make us think about what's important in our lives. ...I now believe that people must slow down, put on the brakes."

Finding your personal balance of time for God, self, work, family and friends is an ever-changing lifetime's work. Discover your current balance. Live it.

Wisdom is as good as an inheritance...the protection of wisdom is like the protection of money....wisdom gives life to the one who possesses it. (Ecclesiastes 7:11, 12)

In silence, Jesus, I listen for Your voice, that I may know Your will.

Shut-Eye Can Be Fatal

When he was in high school, Russell Burris took driver's education classes. "I was told about the importance of a seat belt," he said recently. "I was warned about the dangers of drinking and driving, but no one ever mentioned what could happen if I drove while drowsy."

Shortly after he graduated, he was involved in a car crash after he had not slept in 36 hours. Burris is now a paraplegic.

It's estimated that 20 percent of auto accidents involve sleep-deprived drivers. That's 1.2 million annually. Too many people do not sleep the recommended eight hours.

Especially before a long trip, get a full night's rest. Take frequent breaks and walk around. Listen to talk or information programs on the radio. If you must listen to music, sing along. Consuming some protein and caffeine can help.

Accidents happen, but don't contribute to them by the lack of z-z-z's. Your body and soul will thank you.

Whose offspring are worthy of honor? Human offspring. (Sirach 10:19)

Jesus, Carpenter of Nazareth, You knew how to balance work, prayer and rest. Show me how to do the same.

No More Sitting Back

"People had given, given, given to me for seven years and now I was able to give something back–to help someone in a way that people had helped me," said Doris Jones.

When she heard about the attacks of September 11, 2001, she understood the pain of families who lost loved ones. Her 26-year-old daughter Carrie had been killed in the 1995 bombing of the federal building in Oklahoma City.

Doris Jones joined an American Red Cross group going to New York City. There, she assisted family members as they were escorted to Ground Zero saying, "I could see myself with...the same looks of disbelief. ...My heart broke for them."

When she returned home, she took courses in disaster preparedness, specializing in family services. "(Carrie's) not here now, so maybe I can do things in her honor," says Mrs. Jones. "I'm not one to sit back anymore."

No one should sit back when there's so much to do.

In Joppa there was a disciple whose name was Tabitha, which in Greek is Dorcas. She was devoted to good works and acts of charity. (Acts (:36)

Merciful Lord, grant me the grace to give back, to be generous.

Setting the Lighting

Yousuf Karsh's photographs captured legendary faces of the past century that ranged from George Bernard Shaw to Fidel Castro to Andy Warhol. Even if you don't know Karsh's name, it's likely you've seen some of his celebrated prints.

His portrait of Winston Churchill, taken in 1941, marked a turning point in Karsh's career, despite the fact that he was given only two minutes to take it. Legend has it that Karsh managed to anger the statesman by taking away his cigar. The resulting photograph stunningly captured Churchhill's famed bulldog-like tenacity and immediately shot Karsh to international fame.

Karsh's secret? The careful lighting and composition of his portraits, which as historian Peter Pollock once put it, "transform[ed] the human face into legend."

Sometimes, life is all about perspective. What in your life would change if you looked at it through different lighting?

Do not judge by appearances. (John 7:24)

Help us, Lord, to see all facets of ourselves and those around us.

A Different View

Bonnie is a typical college student. She worked hard to get into an Ivy League school and A-plus papers cover her dorm-sized refrigerator. She spends countless hours just laughing and talking with all the friends she's made. Bonnie works, attends classes, is involved in clubs, and has a good social life. She also deals with one obstacle that most college students don't. Bonnie is blind.

Life as a blind college student isn't always easy. She adapts by using such helpers as a voice-activated computer and a guide dog. Through it all, Bonnie rarely stops smiling. She uses the gifts that she's been given to the fullest extent, instead of focusing on what she doesn't have. "It may not be easy," she says. "But there's nothing I can't do."

A positive attitude creates opportunities that might seem impossible otherwise.

Hoping against hope, (Abraham) believed that he would become 'the father of many nations,' according to what was said. (Romans 4:18)

Help me appreciate the gifts you have given me, Lord.

In Memory of Maria

Maria and Carlos Hernandez waged war against the drug dealers in their Brooklyn, New York, neighborhood. Thanks to their efforts, drug dealing is much reduced.

But the battle cost Maria her life. She was killed by a bullet fired into the couple's apartment.

"I thought of killing them," recalls Carlos of the 1989 shooting. But he quickly realized that his arrest and jail time would leave his three children without a father as well.

Two men, neighborhood drug dealers, are now serving life prison terms for the murder of Maria Hernandez. And Carlos still serves his community, including keeping watch: Keeping watch on activities in the neighborhood park named in honor of his late wife.

"I cherish the good moments I spent with her," says Carlos. "The media attention about her death forced a lot of people to do something positive to clean up our community."

If you don't care for your community, who will?

Act justly. (Jeremiah 7:5)

Strengthen me, Father, so that I may help reveal Your justice in today's world.

The Comfort of Dog Tags

Jim Gain believes a soldier's dog tags are sacred. His father had been in the military and Gain says he and his siblings had to memorize their dad's tag number.

So while on a business trip to Ho Chi Minh City, Vietnam with Rob Stiff, a business associate and friend, the two men stumbled upon a street vendor selling hundreds of military dog tags.

They made a second trip to Vietnam to search for more. They bought 620 American dog tags, and subsequently searched for the tags' original owners or their families. The two have spent $9,000 of their own money and have so far returned 52 tags, but it's been a labor of love, sacrifice and patriotism. The way Stiff sees it, "It's saying 'Thank you' for sacrificing for every bit of freedom we have today."

None of us knows how and in what way we will serve others, but seizing the opportunity is what counts.

Serve one another with whatever gift each of you has received. (1 Peter 4:10)

Help me to reassess and reorder my priorities, Christ Jesus.

Fostering Love

Statistics about children raised in foster care are bleak. According to Anne Cassidy, author of *Parents Who Think Too Much*, 18,000 foster children age out of the system each year. Only half of them graduate from high school. And only 17 percent of these seek higher education. With little emotional or financial support, nearly 40 percent of these won't complete degrees.

The late Joseph Rivers beat the odds. Raised in foster care, he put himself through college, then established the Orphan Foundation of America (OFA) to provide financial support to young adults without parents.

Today his work is carried on by his foster sister, Eileen McCaffrey. Recognizing that encouragement and love were as critical as money, McCaffrey now matches young adults supported by the OFA with caring adults willing to send notes and packages.

Many a life has been turned around by simple acts of generosity.

Judge with justice the cause of the orphan, to make it prosper...defend the rights of the needy. (Jeremiah 5:28)

Open my heart, loving God, to the emotional, spiritual and financial needs of orphans.

Ideas for Change

Sometimes an idea that sounds offbeat is, in fact, on-target. Here are three very different ones that work for the folks involved.

Appointing an official "corporate jester" seemed odd for British Airways. But the company sees that person as the one to question management without fear or repercussion, with criticism couched as harmless jest.

The Navajo National Council decided in 2000, to incorporate *nalyeeh*, the demand that those who have hurt others talk things out, into its justice system. Criminal cases now include a peacemaking session for the parties involved and their families.

Tired of breaking up fights, an elementary school teacher came up with creative conflict resolution. Michael Soth asks his students to re-enact their disagreements. During the "performance" other students can yell "Stop!" and demonstrate alternative responses.

Do you have an idea for an improvement, a solution?

Agree with God and be at peace. (Job 22:21)

Father, light my way in darkness; guide my steps in light.

When "Church is Boring"

There comes a time when many preteens or teens complain about going to church and question their religion. But, writes Susan Alexander Yates, author and mother of five children, "We want our kids to become people of faith."

Precisely because faith will help them deal with life, Yates, writing in *Today's Christian Woman*, says don't ignore their questioning. Youngsters need this spiritual struggle to make their inherited faith their own. Instead, Yates suggests…

• Give good example. Worship every Sunday. Read the Bible.

• Be understanding. Say questioning is okay.

• Be challenging. Provide books. Arrange a meeting with a spiritual guide.

• Find a church that's right for the whole family and insist on attendance unless your teen is exhausted or sick.

• Encourage involvement in an active youth ministry.

Pray for yourself, your family, your world.

The Lord was my support. (Psalm 18:18)

God, be with us as we struggle to understand Your will.

Climbing the Walls

What's driving many American workers up the wall these days? The lack of walls in the workplace.

As many companies seek to cut costs, equalize perks for workers and create a more teamwork-conducive atmosphere, office walls and doors are becoming rare. Some workers can't make the transition to wide open spaces, where privacy and quiet are scarce commodities.

Mary, an experienced sales director, had spent her career in her own office until her most recent position. She "couldn't stand the noise," she admits. Her "ability to focus went down so by Friday, I couldn't concentrate at all." She quit.

Walt, a civil engineer, worked with over 200 people in cloth-covered cubicles. Phone conversations could be overheard. Rumors spread quickly. He remembers the experience with dread.

We all need the serenity and focus of solitude. Spend time alone each day, even if just for five minutes.

**An intelligent person remains silent
(Proverbs 11:12)**

I treasure my time spent communing with You, God. Thank You for each moment of quiet and reflection in my life.

New Hope in "Hospitality City"

Union, South Carolina, has always called itself the "the City of Hospitality." Yet it was in Union, in 1994, that Susan Smith drowned her two young children. Smith initially claimed that an African-American had killed her sons.

Today, thanks to a theater director and his company, a troubled community is on the mend. Richard Geer is the director and creator of a musical called *Turn the Washpot Down,* which focuses on the town's people and history. Geer says proudly, "This is a whole community re-visioning itself, transforming its whole sense of identity."

Union isn't the only place that's benefited from Geer's vision and talents. He's traveled the country, using theater to help cities confront their pasts and presents. Geer says, "I finally made a significant contribution to the world. I am complete."

A life dedicated to healing and helping pays large personal and spiritual dividends.

Blessed are the peacemakers, for they will be called children of God. (Matthew 5:9)

Make me a reconciler, a peace-maker, Abba.

A Blanket of Healing

Barbara Bobrow sits among a circle of women friends. Covered in a patchwork quilt, she pulls the fabric closer, saying, "I feel so protected."

Two years ago, Bobrow was diagnosed with breast cancer. After a mastectomy and chemotherapy, she hoped she was well, but received devastating news: The cancer had spread to her liver.

Bobrow's potential for healing comes not just from medicine but from the love of her friends. From the moment this Connecticut mother of two children received the terrible news, her friends began to create a series of rituals to help her. That included morning quilting bees. Each woman contributed a 7-inch square made from material that was meaningful to her–pieces of wedding gowns, christening dresses, grandma's doilies, things saved from the past.

"This quilt is full of love," Bobrow says. "Each square is so full of life."

Life is best mended with love.

Hold fast to love and justice. (Hosea 12:6)

You hold the plan for us, Master. You weave our lives from the start.

Empower and Inspire

Julie Anne Lobbia had earned an unusual reputation as a tough yet kind investigative reporter. Her death on Thanksgiving morning 2001, after battling ovarian cancer, left many mourning the loss of the reporter who gave "voice to New York's most vulnerable."

Although she wrote memorable, even award-winning articles, she is most remembered for her tenacity in standing up for the little guy. Her mother Julia says, "From the time she was a child...she always wanted to save the world." And for New York's sometimes forgotten poor and immigrant masses, her weekly columns did just that.

Her compassion for those suffering injustice went beyond writing about them. She could be found translating documents for immigrants, volunteering for the Sisters of the Sacred Heart, or caring for friends dying from AIDS.

A city councilman said Julie Anne Lobbia made him feel, "Empowered and inspired."

How does your life empower and inspire others?

My grace is sufficient for you, for power is made perfect in weakness. (2 Corinthians 12:9)

Jesus, may I serve Your people who are most vulnerable.

A Love Feast

One fall afternoon 20 years ago, as she walked to her job as a chef at an Atlantic City, New Jersey, casino, Jean Webster saw a man searching a dumpster for food. She bought the man, John, a cheeseburger, inviting him to her home that evening and many nights after that for a home cooked meal.

Soon John's buddies were stopping by, and Webster made sure all were well-fed. On some days, she fed several hundred people by herself and out of her own pocket. Local churches soon learned of her good deeds and formed The Friends of Jean Webster, building her a commercial kitchen in an old church.

Not in the best of health–22 heart attacks by her tally–Webster vows to keep feeding her friends "until I drop. You gotta do more than feed them," she explains. "You gotta be their mother, sister, friend."

Feed your needy neighbors in body, mind and spirit.

I bent down to them and fed them.
(Hosea 11:4)

I hunger for Your mercy and Your com-passionate care, Father. Do not abandon me.

A Creative Whiz Kid

According to Ryan Patterson, building things "just feels good." In preschool, he was taking apart can openers and stereos to see how they worked. In elementary school he built a robotic floor mop. As a high school senior in Grand Junction, Colorado, Patterson won three prestigious science fairs with his invention of a sign-language translating glove.

Patterson got the idea for the glove after watching a deaf person try to order food at a restaurant through an interpreter. "If I could build an electronic interpreter, it would make life easier for people," he remembers thinking.

Patterson is not a regular kid, insist teachers and students alike. In fact he's "a bit of a rock star." He even used his sign-language translating glove to invite his girlfriend to the senior prom. The way he sees it, "If you're going to have a hobby, you need to have fun with it."

Enjoying what you do leads to happiness.

To each is given a manifestation of the Spirit for the common good. (1 Corinthians 12:7)

May my creativity and abilities benefit others, Christ Jesus.

A Gift to the World

"A wonder should have a profound impact on its population," says Barry Moreno, librarian-historian for the National Park Service in New York. He believes the Statue of Liberty fits the bill.

Its position in New York City's harbor has helped make the 156-ton copper and steel structure a symbol of hope to the world since 1886. It was a gift to America from the people of France.

Writer Alan Solomon met a young man in Morocco who had shared emotional insights into the local political system. Solomon asked what he might send his new friend when he returned to America.

The Moroccan did not hesitate. "Send me," he said, "a post card of the Statue of Liberty."

Prize your liberty and the liberty of all.

For freedom Christ has set us free. Stand firm, therefore, and do not submit again to a yoke of slavery. (Galatians 5:1)

For national treasures, Lord, and symbols that unite us, we thank You.

A "Soapworks" Story

Amylia Antonetti's infant son David was sick. He had allergies. His cheeks and ears were red. He cried incessantly.

One day a picture in a medical book caught her eye. The child looked just like hers. And this child had extreme sensitivity to common household chemicals.

Immediately Antonetti threw out every cleaning product. David's condition quickly improved. But what to use for cleaning? Antonetti's grandmother taught her how to make soap from coconut oil, vinegar, baking soda and soda ash. She used it for everything.

Thinking that other women could use this type of soap, Antonetti looked for a company to manufacture her soap. When the first batch arrived she marketed it to local health-food stores. And, as the saying goes, one thing led to another and today Amylia Antonetti's Soap Works takes in $10 million a year.

That's a reminder that problems are opportunities. Approach them with intelligence and perseverance.

The clever do all things intelligently. (Proverbs 13:16)

Holy Spirit, encourage us to use our intelligence for the good of babies and children.

Transforming Grief into Something Else

When Ken Weaver lost his only son, a 21-year old firefighter, because of the misjudgment of Forest Service supervisors, Weaver turned his grief into lobbying and helped change the standards of accountability.

Devin Weaver's supervisors sent the young man and several other firefighters, three of whom also died, into a blaze on orders that violated or disregarded every one of 10 firefighting safety standards. The elder Weaver and Senator Maria Cantwell of Washington, both of whom have investigated firefighter losses, found stunning similarities between these deaths and others.

Cantwell brought Weaver to the Capitol to address a U.S. Senate committee in support of a bill that would change the way Forest Service deaths are investigated. Weaver's testimony helped pass the bill in Congress and it is now law.

Rather than allowing grief to consume him, Ken Weaver transformed it into help for others. Do all you can to serve.

Be comforted in your grief. (Sirach 38:17)

Help us, Father, to affect positive change no matter the circumstances.

A Kinder, Gentler World

The writer Aldous Huxley once said, "It is amazing to me that, after all these years of study and research, the most important piece of advice I can give is, 'Be a little kinder to one another'."

These words have never seemed more apropos. Many people, these days, are reconnecting with old friends and long-lost relatives; even making amends with enemies. People who haven't communicated in years are sending e-mails and letters, hoping to find a human connection in the midst of our turbulent times.

It's natural to reach for the healing power of human contact. What's more, tragedy reminds us that our time on earth will come to an end.

With what parts of your life would you like to reconnect? While it's impossible to change the past, now might be a good time to reconnect with an old friend, or mend fences with someone you've lost contact with due to differences.

Be reconciled to your brother or sister. (Matthew 5:24)

Father God, help heal Your children. Remind us to reach out to others as a way to heal both them and us.

Following the Sign of the Turkey

It was Thanksgiving Day—the first since brother and sister had lost their mother to a massive stroke.

As Monica prepared dinner for her family and her brother William, she wondered about their mother. As a Christian, she believed her mother was with God—but with her mom's death not even six months' past, she wanted to see some sign that her mother was okay and with her still.

Opening the door to welcome her brother, she found him carrying a "Happy Thanksgiving" sign, complete with a turkey dressed like a pilgrim. "Where did you get that?" Monica asked.

"I found it in the driveway as I was leaving to come over here," William answered.

Here was Monica's sign with the lesson that we have to look, really look, at the things around us. Sometimes the answers to our wonderings and worries are just waiting for us to find them.

The glory of the stars is the beauty of heaven, a glittering array in the heights of the Lord. ...the rainbow...is exceedingly beautiful. It encircles the sky with its glorious arc. (Sirach 43:9, 11)

In sunshine, in rain, in moon-glow and in the stars' beauty, I see signs of Your love for us, Creator.

What's the Good Word?

According to Boaz Keysar, a University of Chicago psychology professor, we often overestimate how well we get our point across when speaking. Here's expert advice to reduce confusion.

- Don't rely on such cues as nodding, making eye contact or saying "uh-huh." They're easy to misinterpret as signs of understanding.

- Train the editor in your head. Stop. Run the phrases through "thought-check" in your head. Be sure what you say is very clear.

- Using questions like "How does that sound?" or "Does that make sense?" Ask listeners to restate your message.

- Listen well. Ask questions. Speakers aren't responsible for the whole exchange.

It's so easy for misunderstandings to occur, even when we are striving for clarity. Take the time to communicate well.

Pay attention to what you hear. (Mark 4:24)

I offer You praise this day, Creator, for You give us everything good.

Cash in Exchange for Service

"We live in a world of abundance, with an inadequate distribution system," say Kevin Ryan and Joel Hodroff. To help change that, the pair launched Community HeroCard, a credit card-like system that rewards volunteers who work for nonprofit programs.

Prospective volunteers purchase a HeroCard from a participating organization. They then use the card to make a purchase at a participating merchant. Half of the reward is deposited as cash into the purchaser's account; an equal sum is deposited once the cardholder completes his or her volunteer activity.

Is paying people to volunteer a good idea? Proponents say that since free time is scarce for most people, it's an innovative way to encourage civic engagement. Ryan hopes to replicate the program around the country. "We have a core belief," he says, "that communities are strongest when they are built and nurtured by the people who live in them."

Support your neighbors with your time and efforts.

Do not neglect to do good. (Hebrews 13:16)

Help me find ways to better connect with my community, God.

Addressing God

Barbara Bartocci wrote her first letter to God in the midst of a heated argument with her husband. An author and motivational speaker, she has penned many letters to the Lord over the years, advocating the practice for others as well.

"It's so easy to live life the way I drive down a familiar road, in a sort of auto-pilot trance, so caught up in my daily busy-ness that I stay asleep to deeper meanings, or the ways in which small choices add up to large outcomes in my life," she explains. "Writing to God slows me down, pulls me over, wakes me up. It's as if God enters my consciousness, not to give me answers but to give me the grace to find the answers that are already there. "

That's a wonderful point. Prayer is a time of discovery, a time to truly learn about God and about ourselves. And the more quiet time you spend with Him, the more you'll find the "answers that are already there."

Guard me, O Lord. (Psalm 140:4)

Author of all life, give me the strength to face the challenges of this day.

Showing Art in Russia

The commitment of a lifetime can make a difference.

Communism fell, the Soviet Union collapsed, but Irina Antonova stayed the director of Moscow's Pushkin Museum of Fine Arts. Her career began one month before the end of World War II and survived Stalinism, unresolved disputes over looted and lost art, state suppression of certain art styles and democracy.

It was on Antonova's watch that the Pushkin went from a secondary museum to a world-class one showcasing major artists.

In addition she and the Russian pianist Sviatoslav Richter organized concerts at the museum every December. They became the most sought-after tickets in Moscow.

"I had no idea it would be for my whole life," Antonova says of her time as Director of the Pushkin. The world of art, however, is surely the better for her lifelong commitment.

Don't be afraid to commit yourself to doing good.

What goodness and beauty are His! (Zechariah 9:17)

In the art of Your creation, Lord, I see Your beauty and love and I praise You.

So, L A U G H !

Humor is both God's gift and a life-saving medicine. A Christopher friend with a keen sense of the absurd and humorous offers some examples:

The Hundred Years War lasted 100 years, right? No, 116 years.

Panama hats come from Panama: nope, Ecuador!

Well, you say, cats must be the source of the catgut formerly used in surgery. Sorry, despite its name, catgut comes from sheep and horses!

In the same vein...

Russians celebrate their October Revolution in November.

Chinese gooseberries come from New Zealand.

That sparrow-sized singer, the purple finch, is actually crimson.

And camel's hair brushes are made of squirrel fur, not camel's.

So, have a laugh. Humor is a health-giving remedy for what ails you.

There is a season, and a time for every matter under heaven...a time to laugh...a time to dance ...a time to embrace. (Ecclesiastes 3:1,4,5)

God, bless me with a keen sense of humor.

Tis the Season for Credit Card Bills

Holiday spending habits leaving you with overdue bills? Paying bills for months after the holidays? Here are a few tips to reduce holiday debt:

- List all your spending categories: gifts; wrapping, postage, Christmas cards, special foods or crafts, travel, etc. Note the amount of money you plan to spend for each category. This, totaled, is your holiday expense amount. If the sum is more than your available cash, start pruning your list.

- At the end of the day empty change from purchases from purses and pockets. Save it for gifts.

- Re-think spending habits like the daily latte. Skip it a few days a week and save the money.

- Consider moonlighting, doing overtime or having a weekend job.

- Crash save, eliminate all but necessities, for a few weeks.

Above all, remember it's the love and the thought behind the gift and the season that count, not the value of the gift.

Love builds up. (1 Corinthians 8:1)

Jesus, so many use Your birthday as a reason to focus on money and gifts. Help me focus on You each and every Christmas.

Asking For Help

Darlene and Dale Emme endured one of the most tragic events parents can experience: the suicide of a teenage child. Even though their 17-year-old son Michael left a note telling his family it wasn't their fault, the Emmes insist they learned that "suicide is not about being stupid or selfish, it's about pain."

When people asked them what they could do for them, they would say that if ever someone was in that much pain, to ask for help. The Emmes had that thought printed on bright yellow paper to give out at Michael's memorial.

They began the Yellow Ribbon Suicide Prevention Program and the Light for Life Foundation to aid troubled teens. The programs give out business cards with a yellow ribbon on it with the words "This ribbon is a lifeline." Today, there are 80 official chapters in the United States and in 47 countries.

Out of their sorrow, Dale and Darlene Emme found a way to offer other parents' children a lifeline. Who needs your lifeline?

(Jesus) cried with a loud voice, "Lazarus, come out!" ...Jesus said to them, "Unbind him, and let him go." (John 11:43,44)

In my hour of extreme distress, Lord, help me.

What's On Inside?

Developing an interior life happens in different ways for different people, but Dan Andriacco, director of the Office of Communications for the Catholic Archdiocese of Cincinnati, points out that evaluating the role television and other electronic media play in our lives is important to the process.

"To step away from the electronic media for awhile is not to tune them out, but to (decrease)... their role in our lives," he observes. "Turning on the TV shouldn't be an automatic activity but a decision."

Andriacco suggests "fasting" from electronic media one or two days a week for a period of time, such as during Advent or Lent. But he urges people to go beyond "giving up" television as a sacrifice. "It is not so much a giving up as an opening up," he writes, "to God, God's world, and God's people."

Nurturing your interior or spiritual life is vital to your well-being. Make time for your relationship with God.

The heavens are telling the glory of God; and the firmament proclaims His handiwork. (Psalm 19:1)

Remind me how important it is to listen for Your still small voice at every moment of every day, God.

Girls, Sports and Success

"Athletics teach you tenacity, discipline and social skills," says tennis great Tracy Austin.

Research proves that athletic girls and young women have high self-esteem, do better academically, don't abuse drugs, become pregnant or smoke and are better able to handle life's ups and downs.

"Girls still face an uphill battle embracing sports and overcoming cultural stereotypes," says Mary Jo Kane, director of the Tucker Center for Research on Girls and Women. "But if parents give their daughters a consistent message that sports is good for them, too, then they grow up believing this is natural."

Parents, support your daughters. Being strong and athletic is not only feminine, it's healthful. Set a good example for all your children with a health enhancing exercise program of your own.

Encourage all young people to develop all their abilities.

I commend to you our sister Phoebe, a deacon of the church at Cenchrae....Greet Prisca and Aquila who work with me. ...Greet Mary, who has worked very hard among you. (Romans 16:1, 3, 6)

Jesus who respected women, help us end discrimination against women.

Give Credit Where It's Due

There are many times when people do useful and helpful things for which they receive little or no credit. That's life. But it's also nice when someone receives long overdue recognition.

Bill Gates and Steve Jobs are known to many beyond the world of computing. Not so Dr. Ed Roberts.

But H. Edward Roberts is an acknowledged founding father of the personal computing industry. He made significant contributions before leaving to study and practice medicine. A physician in Georgia, he's fulfilled in this second career.

Although over the years, others have been credited with inventing the PC, or personal computer, technology historian Paul E. Ceruzzi lists Ed Roberts as an important founder of the industry.

Try to notice the nice things others do for you and give them credit as well as thanks.

Judge your neighbor's feelings by your own. (Sirach 31:15)

Remind me, Lord, to recognize the contributions of others.

A Holiday Primer

Kerry LaBounty, a personal and business coach, offers these tips for a happier holiday season.

- Don't "should" yourself. "Shoulds" are based on internal pressures or others' agendas.
- Change your gift-giving practice. Instead of expensive gifts, donate to charity.
- Take time to free your mind from "obligations." Soak up the beauties of the season instead.
- Change your attitude. You don't control every aspect of your life, but you do control how you react. Choose to be happy.
- Be grateful. Oh, not for anything specific, but for everything. You will experience an abundance of joy.
- Be kind and patient. Perhaps not a first response, genuine kindness tends to multiply. And, you are making the world better.

Be patient with the world - and start with yourself.

Clothe yourselves with compassion, kindness, humility, meekness and patience. (Colossians 3:12)

Fill me with the peace that comes from knowing You, Abba.

A Family Says Thank You

Along with the rest of the their family, Mike and Tim Ross are thankful for the anonymous organ donor whose liver saved the life of their youngest sister.

On the ten-year anniversary the brothers decided to roller ski across Canada in order to raise awareness about the special and heroic role played by organ donors and their loved ones and to show their gratitude.

At various stops along the way they spoke about transplantation and met others touched by this issue. Sometimes the occasion was bittersweet, as donor families were reminded of their loss while also seeing evidence of how much the gift of life meant to others.

"I guess initiating this is just a first step," said Tim. "I really hope that this would inspire others to get out there and do the same thing, thanking these families for their decision."

Show gratitude to all who change your life for the better.

Be generous. (Judges 21:22)

God, thank You for the many blessings bestowed upon our families. May we remain ever grateful.

Spending Christmas in Bed

Seven months pregnant, Lian Dolan was determined to give her two-year-old son Brookes a wonderful Christmas. But after she went into preterm labor on the Thanksgiving weekend, the only plans she made involved complete bed rest.

Called off were the baking, shopping and craft-making. Called in were family and friends to assist Berick Dolan in looking after his wife and son. Happily, a healthy baby boy, Colin, was born on February 2, two weeks *late*.

The help Lian Dolan received from so many people gave her a "tremendous debt to repay." "Now when I hear about a sick friend, a new baby or a death in the family, I am there on the front steps, pan of food in hand," she says.

That time also made her re-write her holiday plans forever. "I don't buy as many gifts," she explains. "Instead, I try to appreciate the ones I already have."

Mary...went with haste to...the house of Zechariah and greeted Elizabeth. When Elizabeth heard Mary's greeting, the child leaped in her womb. ...Mary remained with her about three months and then returned to her home. (Luke 1:39, 40-41, 56)

In my neighbor, Lord, help me to see and serve You.

All Treats, No Tricks

A treat is a reward for doing something well or avoiding something unhealthy or unhelpful. It is also the opportunity to reconnect with your self. Try to treat yourself every few months to a special weekend:

• Gather everybody for a family picnic or party.

• Spend a weekend away with your spouse.

• Ignore every chore to spend a few days reading or writing.

• Sleep as much as you want when you want.

• Take a spontaneous, unplanned, clock-free few days.

But whatever way you decide to treat yourself, look at it as an opportunity to invest in yourself for your own good and the good of your loved ones.

No one can keep giving if there is nothing left to give.

If one is mean to himself, to whom will he be generous? He will not enjoy his own riches. No one is worse than one who is grudging to himself. (Sirach 14:5-6)

Thank you, Creator, for my being. Show me how to nourish myself for my good and the good of others.

The Nose Knows

While only three of our 100,000 genes control our color vision, 1,000 are responsible for our sense of smell.

One example of a scent with thousands of years of history is frankincense. It is derived from the gum resin of a tree grown in only a few areas of Asia and Africa, and has traditionally been used for embalming and religious ceremonies. It is also an herbal remedy for problems from skin conditions to colds to bad breath.

However, it was not until 1983 that the medicinal powers of frankincense were proved in clinical trials. It can reduce painful rheumatic swelling and ease symptoms of the related Crohn's disease.

Nature is filled with wonders for us to discover and use in a variety of ways. Appreciate everything God has provided for us.

Opening their treasure chests, they offered Him gifts of gold, frankincense, and myrrh. (Matthew 2:11)

Lord, thank You for the natural wonders You have placed in this world.

Has Tech Wrecked Our Relationships?

We can be connected 24-hours a day, yet our personal interactions with our extended families seem to be fading. The days of dropping in on neighbors, friends and relatives has given way to cell phones and e-mail, but at what cost?

Our larger family defines us; places our lives in context of the greater life story; and teaches children what we believe in, what we stand for, who we are and thereby who they are.

Probably since the beginning of time, children have tuned out much of what parents try to teach them. However, friends, grandparents, and aunts and uncles can pass along important traditions and values in a subtle way that can have a major impact on children's lives. Without realizing it they will be taught something about their family, about themselves, about life.

Who teaches your children who you are?

Keep My teachings as the apple of your eye. (Proverbs 7:2)

Jesus, help me overcome physical distance and stay close to those I love.

Anyone for a Christmas Swim?

If December holidays are getting too tense for you and yours, there are any number of solutions you might consider.

According to *Good Housekeeping* magazine, many "are rewriting the rules that confine the Christmas spirit to the last month of the year." Some families make plans to get together with others in January in order to simplify December commitments. Some have chosen Valentine's Day for their belated celebrations.

Others, like the family of Lisa Birenbaum, have even opted for a date in July. Better weather, opportunities for large groups to meet outdoors and less hectic schedules make for a more enjoyable gathering. Her family selects a different country each year for their theme and creates food and decorations around it. Says Birenbaum, "We have fun finding recipes and creating the look of the party."

Use your imagination to make the holidays happy for all.

Rejoice in God's mercy. (Sirach 51:29)

Give us the love and courage needed to think "outside the box" when necessary, Lord.

What's the Good Word?

According to Webster's dictionary, euphemisms are agreeable or inoffensive expressions substituted for ones that may offend or suggest something unpleasant. Perhaps every age has been rich in them, but ours seems especially so. Here are a few:

- *unacknowledged repetitions; derivative passages* = plagiarism
- *job survivor* = person not yet right sized, attrited, or managed down
- *involuntary normal attrition* = laying off workers
- *problem-plagued* = drug-addled
- *post-verdict response* = riot
- *poorly buffered precipitation* = acid rain
- *mandatory discontinued attendance* = suspension of a student from classes
- *duty-not-paid importing* = smuggling

If these and other expressions add color to daily speech, that's good. But if they impede clarity and truthfulness, that's bad. Choose your words well and wisely.

Put away from you crooked speech...devious talk. (Proverbs 4:24)

Holy Spirit, inspire me to truthful and intelligent speech.

Angels in Waiting

Country singer Tammy Cochran hit the top ten with *Angels in Waiting.* Listeners connected with the message she shared after losing two brothers to cystic fibrosis.

Cochran has received over 10,000 notes from people telling her how much the song has meant to them. But it did not come easily. Even before she signed a record deal, Cochran knew she wanted to write a song that would honor the memory of her brothers. But after struggling with her emotions and the words for more than a year, she finally turned to two co-writers for help in capturing the right message.

"They were angels in waiting," they wrote, "Waiting for wings/To fly from this world/ Away from their pain/ Treasuring time/ Till time came to leave/ Leaving behind/ Sweet memories."

Next time you find yourself spinning your wheels, reach out to a friend. A fresh perspective may be all you need.

Blessed are they who mourn, for they will be comforted. (Matthew 5:4)

Lord, bless us with courage.

Angel of Marye's Heights

In December 1862, frustrating delays prevented Union forces from securing the heights above Fredericksburg, Virginia, causing one of the worst Union losses of the American Civil War.

When the fighting ended, nearly 6,300 Union casualties lay along a stone wall, which had protected Confederate riflemen.

By the next morning, 19-year-old South Carolinian Richard Kirkland could no longer bear the cries of the dying. He gathered canteens of water, hopped over the wall and through a shower of Union bullets ministered to the wounded. For nearly two hours, Kirkland made trips over the stone wall to comfort the "enemy."

His brigade commander, General J. B. Kershaw, wrote, "Who shall say how sweet his rest that Winter's night. ...He has bequeathed...to the world an example which dignified our common humanity."

Indeed, how sweet the rest of those who help others in their time of need, no matter the risk.

**Sweet is the sleep of laborers.
(Ecclesiastes 5:12)**

Help us to learn compassion, Merciful One.

The Playing Field of Life

Star quarterback John Elway retired from the National Football League in 1999. For 16 years everything had revolved around winning the Super Bowl.

Then, in the span of a few years, Elway suffered business reversals; the deaths of his twin sister and his father; and separation from Janet, his wife of 18 years and the mother of their four kids. "When you're the quarterback, you're in control," he said. "Now, things go wrong and I don't have the football."

Elway courted Janet, going to the mall with her and the kids. Soon, the family was under one roof again. He's making a real effort to put them first from now on. "I'm trying to do things that make me content, things that aren't necessarily about achieving," Elway says.

Perhaps he would agree with the philosopher Lin Yutang who wrote that "contentment is knowing how to enjoy what you have...losing all desire for things beyond your reach."

Be content with what you have. (Hebrews 13:5)

Help me understand the value of contentment as well as achievement, Holy Wisdom.

Think Getting a Shot is Bad?

Christina Santhouse was eight years old when she was diagnosed with Rasmussen's encephalitis, an autoimmune disorder that eventually leads to severe retardation. Doctors treated the disease with its only known cure: a hemispherectomy, the removal of the diseased right half of Christina's brain. That was the only way to stop the more than 100 seizures a day that Christina had had as a result of her illness.

The young girl underwent a surgery that lasted for nearly 14 hours. Luckily, due to her youth, the remaining hemisphere of Christina's brain assumed the functions of the lost half. Christina, now a healthy teenager, reports partial paralysis on her left side and loss of peripheral vision in her left eye. She says that despite occasional weak moments, she feels it happened to her for a reason.

Faith and confidence can do wonders in the face of adversity. Trust yourself to endure.

Though I walk through the darkest valley, I fear no evil; for You are with me. (Psalm 23:4)

Help us, Lord, to have the courage and determination to face even seemingly insurmountable odds.

When Youngsters Talk Back

Children always test their parents' limits. It's just part of growing up. That includes the way they talk back to mom and dad.

What's a parent to do? Dr. T. Berry Brazelton, a Harvard Medical School professor, offers these suggestions:

- Take the high road. Children are more respectful of control in an adult after losing self-control themselves, so don't lash out.

- Don't take the sassy remarks personally and do take the time to regain your composure before addressing the behavior calmly and directly.

- Make it clear this way of speaking is not acceptable in your household. A time-out or a grounding may be appropriate punishment.

- Remember that discipline, when administered with love and compassion, is a gift. It says to the child, "I'm here to protect you, even from yourself!"

We all need self-discipline. It's part of being mature.

We had human parents to discipline us, and we respected them. (Hebrews 12:9)

Please, Lord, guide parents in the proper and loving discipline of their children. Help mothers and fathers see discipline as a way to help, not hurt, their children.

Tolling Bells

A woman heading for a Christmas Open House at the National Cathedral in Washington, D.C. parked her car several blocks away—and couldn't find the cathedral. Then the tolling bells guided her.

Like most church bells, the bells of the National Cathedral's Kibbey Carillon ring out in times of joy, sorrow and celebration; as well as during services. The set of 53 bells is the third heaviest in the world, the largest of them weighing twelve tons, the smallest, only seventeen pounds.

During a renovation the carillon's original manufacturers, John Taylor Bell Foundry of England, were called on to replace badly worn clappers and to regrind others. Cathedral craftsman did needed sanding, priming and painting.

All worked together to ensure that these bells will continue to "draw people toward the Cathedral"—and to God.

Praise (the Lord) with trumpet...lute and harp!
Praise Him with tambourine...strings and pipe!
Praise Him with clanging cymbals!
(Psalm 150:3-5)

Father, draw our attention to all of Your glories.

In Our Parents' Best Interest

As parents age and become infirm, many grown children question how best to help. Some, like editor Gilda Caserta, take ailing parents into their own home. Her widowed mother, who has dementia and diabetes, lives with her.

"I've sacrificed full-time work to arrange my schedule around her needs. I watch my expenses closely. But I couldn't look into her fading hazel-green eyes," said Caserta, "and not try to make her golden years as bright as they could be."

According to Gail Hunt, executive director of the National Alliance for Caregiving, "eighty percent of the care provided to older people in this country is provided free by family and friends."

Caregiving is demanding, so know your limits and get support. You will not truly help your parents if you hurt yourself emotionally, physically or financially. Very sick, frail parents may need the round-the-clock care offered in nursing homes.

As in all decisions, use your heart <u>and</u> your head.

Honor your father and your mother.
(Matthew 15:4)

Father, watch over Your children – of all ages.

One Moment at a Time

Doug Bloch was no stranger to depression when, at 47, the disease threatened to overwhelm him. Physically ill and in the midst of a painful divorce, he didn't want to interact with friends or family; nor could he focus on work.

After psychiatric hospitalization and medication, Bloch went to a clinic for group and individual therapy from 9 to 3:30 five days a week. A nurse there, herself a recovering alcoholic, suggested Alcoholics Anonymous' "24-hour plan. Instead of looking at the long term, we focus on one day at a time," she said.

So, Bloch started to take better care of himself physically; reached out to friends and neighbors; worked at replacing negative thoughts with positive ones; looked for small blessings; prayed and asked others to pray for him.

That's a good example for anyone. Focus on one day at a time and you'll be better able to cope with life.

The Lord is my shepherd. (Psalm 23:1)

Thank you God, for each precious moment of my life.

The Bear Essentials

Some people are never too young to do good for others. Caitlin Phelan of Ipswich, Mass. was only 8 when, after watching news footage of homeless children on Christmas Day, she told her mother, Robin, that she had to help. They promised each other they'd make a difference.

Holding her favorite teddy bear, Caitlin mused, "If this comforts me, it must comfort other children." Inspired, Robin Phelan began the Teddy Bear Foundation Inc., to donate stuffed toys to needy kids in the Boston area.

More than 9,000 bears have been distributed. While donations of money and bears arrive from all over, the letters that mean the most to the Phelans come from kids like Jimmy. He wrote, "Thank you for my new friend. I will never let him go."

Because of a then 8-year-old child's desire to help, despairing kids are finding small comforts. You're never too young or too old to reach out to those in need.

Let the little children come to Me...for it is to such as these that the kingdom of heaven belongs. (Matthew 19:14)

Lord Jesus, inspire me to extend myself to those who crave comfort.

Stopping Stress

Here are 12 steps to less stress, even during the most tension-filled days:

- Practice replacing a stressful activity with something positive.
- Exercise.
- Play music.
- Breathe deeply.
- Practice saying, "No," as a way of setting priorities.
- Limit time with negative people because they drain energy.
- Adjust expectations. Expect life to be messy so you'll be more likely to be content with the simple blessings God sends to you.
- Develop healthy sleeping habits.
- Laugh often.
- Choose daily to follow God. Make quiet times to hear His voice.

We do not determine everything that happens to us. Yet we always get to choose our response.

Oh that You would bless me...and...keep me from hurt and harm! (1 Chronicles 4:10)

Master, You are the source of wisdom and strength.

The Boy who Became Santa

Harold Neumeister's dad terrorized and abused him and his mother. As an adult, booze and drugs led Neumeister to lose everything–wife, kids, job and home.

Although he doesn't remember how, Neumeister found his way to Tender Mercies, an agency that provides housing for the homeless. With help from counselors, he eventually got a job.

One day his employer asked the now white-haired and white-bearded Neumeister to play Santa at the annual Christmas party for needy children. He said, "Yes," then and in the years since.

As he listened to the children on his lap, Neumeister found he could help create the Christmases he had once longed for and never had. "The enjoyment they feel–they give it back to me," he says. "As Santa, I can be something I never was."

Deep inside our dreams still live, waiting for us to give them wings.

Let the little children come to Me, and do not stop them; for it is to such as these that the kingdom of heaven belongs. (Matthew 19:14)

Abba, O Father, protect children in emotionally and physically abusive homes.

An Unexpected Christmas

Don Graves's father remembers a holiday morning in the early 1920s as one of the "finest Christmases we ever had."

The family business had gone under and jobs were scarce. An economic downturn had taken its toll, and the Graves simply couldn't afford Christmas presents that year.

Yet when they awoke that Christmas morning, the tree was surrounded with gifts. Their mother–Don Graves's grandmother–unwrapped a shawl she had lost months earlier. Don's father got a hat he thought he had left in a restaurant in November. A sister got her old slippers and a brother, a pair of patched trousers.

For months, Don's uncle Morris had been hiding away things he knew wouldn't be missed by his family members. Because of his ingenuity, the entire family had presents to open that Christmas morning.

In what may seem to be the worst of times, the human spirit and intellect lift others up. How can you reflect that in your life?

A cheerful heart has a continual feast. (Proverbs 15:15)

Lord, help us to find and share the positive in any situation.

Fostering a Community

Brenda Krause Eheart, a home economist with a doctorate in child development, was appalled by the state of the foster care system in much of the United States. She persuaded Illinois lawmakers to give her nonprofit group, Generations of Hope, a $1 million start-up grant. Her idea: create a community for foster kids and senior citizens.

After purchasing a decommissioned Air Force training base from the Pentagon, Eheart built Hope Meadows, a unique neighborhood of 56 split-level homes with a playground and a community center. The 11 families and 56 surrogate grandparents are parents to 47 adopted, foster and biological children.

While receiving many awards and much media coverage, Hope Meadows' real success is in the bonds between the old and the young, many of whom have suffered severe abuse and neglect. One senior said, "We have the best of both worlds here. Every day, little miracles happen."

Miracles do happen, but not without faith and work.

**Do not repay anyone evil for evil.
(Romans 12:17)**

With love and support, Loving Lord, healing is possible.

What's Right with Youth

Peter Benson, president of the Search Institute, maintains that there are 40 basic "assets" which help kids grow up happy and healthy. He pinpointed these assets by asking one million happy, well-adjusted kids nationwide about themselves.

Here are a few "assets:"

• A family that provides love and support
• Encouragement to do his/her best
• Neighbors who show they care
• Friendships with adults other than parents
• Weekly exposure to the arts
• A safe home, school and neighborhood
• That his/her life "has purpose"
• Positive and responsible adults

The more "assets" kids have, the less likely they are to engage in anti-social, dangerous behavior. There's no magic in that. It's just caring and common sense.

Jesus said, "Let the little children come to Me...for it is to such as these that the kingdom of heaven belongs." (Matthew 19:14)

God, help adults realize that children are a precious gift to the world.

But I'm a Christian!

"I'd always thought Christians could never be child abusers," says Kathy Collard Miller, an international speaker and author of books on spiritual growth and parenting.

Through her Bible study group, Miller discovered that the impatience she experienced with her toddler, Darcy, was actually rooted in anger she felt towards her husband. She also realized her expectations of marriage were unrealistic.

"Only God can meet all my needs," says Miller. Today, she and her husband are celebrating more than 30 years of married life, and she and her daughter, now age 24, have a close and loving relationship.

Miller recognized her weakness, sought help, and took steps to correct it. Her misguided notion that Christians could never be child abusers could apply to any situation.

Accept your humanity, seek help, and keep beginning anew. Trust God. He has faith in you—whatever your faith.

God the Lord is my strength. (Habakkuk 3:19)

Lord, remind me that spirituality does not exempt me from the human race, from human problems. Help me lean on You.

Learning From Jake

Jake Porter spent three years on the McDermott, Ohio, Northwest High School football team, yet he barely stepped onto the field. Porter suffers from chromosomal fragile X syndrome, a cause of mental retardation, but that never stopped him from attending team practices.

And that's why when Jake scored a touchdown for his school at the very end of an otherwise losing effort there was national attention. Derek Dewitt, coach of the opposing Waverly, Ohio team insisted that Porter run for the end zone. In effect, Jake had 21 teammates cheering him on and helping him score.

The best part of the story is that the people in both Waverly and McDermott seem to be treating each other better, and kids in the schools walk around beaming.

Though Jake Porter can barely write or read, he's teaching others by his positive, enthusiastic example.

Are you?

I have set you an example. (John 13:15)

May I be open to learning from everyone, Creator.

Thank Goodness!

Mary Jane Ryan's father lay in a hospital bed, dying of emphysema. Yet when asked, "How do you feel, Dad?" he replied, "Life is good. I love watching the ball game on TV and I love reading the comics."

Noting his emphasis on what he was enjoying rather than all he had lost, Ryan was reminded of the freedom we have to choose our approach to life.

"Our spiritual task is to move beyond a purely emotional response to life and cultivate positive emotions as habits of the heart," says Ryan, author of *Attitudes of Gratitude*.

She encourages parents to train the next generation to think positively. Steer away from telling children about all the things for which they "should" be grateful, she suggests. Instead, ask little ones to name a few things they are grateful for at the end of each day.

It's an exercise that would benefit us all.

With gratitude in your hearts sing...to God. (Colossians 3:16)

Thank You, good Lord, thank You.

Lost on a Mountain

Decades may separate us from the experience 12-year-old Donn Fendler had in 1939, but the miraculous story of the nine days he spent lost on a Maine mountain is no less compelling today.

Leaving the summit of Mount Katahdin, the boy became disoriented. Believing he would soon come upon the camp where his father and brother waited, he ended up hiking nearly 50 miles through rough and dangerous terrain. Sleet and winds pelted him on and off throughout his ordeal. He dealt with hallucinations, terror, exhaustion and bears. He survived on wild strawberries and water from the stream he followed.

Yet he never lost faith. Seeking out soft patches of moss each day, Donn Fendler bent his swollen, bug-bitten knees and prayed daily for his family, for food, and for his safe return. Finally, rescue came.

We never know our own strength and courage until they are tested, but we can nurture our faith and character each day.

He will command His angels...to guard you in all your ways. (Psalm 91:11)

Inspire me to persevere, Lord God.

Also Available

Have you enjoyed volume 38 of *Three Minutes a Day*? These other Christopher offerings may interest you:

- **News Notes** – published ten times a year on a variety of topics of current interest. One copy as published is free; bulk and standing orders may be arranged.

- **Ecos Cristóforos** – Spanish translations of selected News Notes. Issued six times a year. One copy as published is free; bulk and standing orders may be placed.

- **Wall or Desk Appointment Calendar and Monthly Planner** – The calendar offers an inspirational message for each day as well as for each month. The Monthly Planner with its trim, practical design also offers a monthly inspirational message.

- **Videocassettes** – Christopher videocassettes range from wholesome entertainment to serious discussions of family life and current social and spiritual issues.

For more information on The Christophers or to receive **News Notes, Ecos Cristóforos** or fulfillment brochures write:

The Christophers
12 East 48th Street
New York, NY 10017

Phone: 212-759-4050

Web site: www.christophers.org

E-mail: mail@christophers.org

The Christophers is a non-profit media organization founded in 1945. We share the message of personal responsibility and service to God and humanity with people of all faiths and no particular faith. Gifts are welcome and tax-deductible. Our legal title for wills is The Christophers, Inc.